Octavio Paz

CONSULTING EDITORS

Octavio Paz

Joseph Roman

CHELSEA HOUSE PUBLISHERS
NEW YORK ■ PHILADELPHIA

CHELSEA HOUSE PUBLISHERS

Editorial Director: Richard Rennert
Executive Managing Editor: Karyn Gullen Browne
Executive Editor: Sean Dolan
Copy Chief: Robin James
Picture Editor: Adrian G. Allen
Art Director: Robert Mitchell
Manufacturing Director: Gerald Levine
Systems Manager: Lindsey Ottman
Production Coordinator: Marie Claire Cebrián-Ume

HISPANICS OF ACHIEVEMENT
Senior Editor: Philip Koslow

Staff for OCTAVIO PAZ
Designer: M. Cambraia Magalhaes
Picture Researcher: Lisa Kirshner
Cover Illustrator: Daniel O'Leary

First Printing

1   3   5   7   9   8   6   4   2

Library of Congress Cataloging-in-Publication Data
Roman, Joseph.
Octavio Paz/Joseph Roman.
p. cm.—(Hispanics of achievement)
Includes bibliographical references and index.
Summary: Presents the life and career of the Mexican poet.
ISBN 0-7910-1249-2
0-7910-1276-X (pbk.)
1. Paz, Octavio, 1914– —Juvenile literature. 2. Poets, Mexican—20th century—
Biography—Juvenile literature. [1. Paz, Octavio, 1914– . 2. Poets, Mexican.] I. Title.
II. Series.
92-47051
PQ7297.P285Z9614 1993
CIP
861—dc20
[B]
AC

CONTENTS

HISPANICS OF ACHIEVEMENT

JOAN BAEZ
Mexican-American folksinger

RUBÉN BLADES
Panamanian lawyer and entertainer

JORGE LUIS BORGES
Argentine writer

PABLO CASALS
Spanish cellist and conductor

MIGUEL DE CERVANTES
Spanish writer

CESAR CHAVEZ
Mexican-American labor leader

JULIO CÉSAR CHÁVEZ
Mexican boxing champion

EL CID
Spanish military leader

HENRY CISNEROS
Mexican-American political leader

ROBERTO CLEMENTE
Puerto Rican baseball player

SALVADOR DALÍ
Spanish painter

PLÁCIDO DOMINGO
Spanish singer

GLORIA ESTEFAN
Cuban-American singer

GABRIEL GARCÍA MÁRQUEZ
Colombian writer

FRANCISCO JOSÉ DE GOYA
Spanish painter

JULIO IGLESIAS
Spanish singer

RAUL JULIA
Puerto Rican actor

FRIDA KAHLO
Mexican painter

JOSÉ MARTÍ
Cuban revolutionary and poet

RITA MORENO
Puerto Rican singer and actress

PABLO NERUDA
Chilean poet and diplomat

OCTAVIO PAZ
Mexican poet and critic

PABLO PICASSO
Spanish artist

ANTHONY QUINN
Mexican-American actor

DIEGO RIVERA
Mexican painter

LINDA RONSTADT
Mexican-American singer

ANTONIO LÓPEZ DE SANTA ANNA
Mexican general and politician

GEORGE SANTAYANA
Spanish philosopher and poet

JUNÍPERO SERRA
Spanish missionary and explorer

LEE TREVINO
Mexican-American golfer

PANCHO VILLA
Mexican revolutionary

CHELSEA HOUSE PUBLISHERS

HISPANICS OF ACHIEVEMENT

Rodolfo Cardona

The Spanish language and many other elements of Spanish culture are present in the United States today and have been since the country's earliest beginnings. Some of these elements have come directly from the Iberian Peninsula; others have come indirectly, by way of Mexico, the Caribbean basin, and the countries of Central and South America.

Spanish culture has influenced America in many subtle ways, and consequently many Americans remain relatively unaware of the extent of its impact. The vast majority of them recognize the influence of Spanish culture in America, but they often do not realize the great importance and long history of that influence. This is partly because Americans have tended to judge the Hispanic influence in the United States in statistical terms rather than to look closely at the ways in which individual Hispanics have profoundly affected American culture. For this reason, it is fitting that Americans obtain more than a passing acquaintance with the origins of these Spanish cultural elements and gain an understanding of how they have been woven into the fabric of American society.

It is well documented that Spanish seafarers were the first to explore and colonize many of the early territories of what is today called the United States of America. For this reason, students of geography discover Hispanic names all over the map of the United States. For instance, the Strait of Juan de Fuca was named after the Spanish explorer who first navigated the waters of the Pacific Northwest; the names of states such as Arizona (arid zone), Montana (mountain), Florida (thus named because it was reached on Easter Sunday, which in Spanish is called the feast of Pascua Florida), and California (named after a fictitious land in one of the first and probably the most popular among the Spanish novels of chivalry, *Amadis of Gaul*) are all derived from Spanish; and there are numerous mountains, rivers, canyons, towns, and cities with Spanish names throughout the United States.

Not only explorers but many other illustrious figures in Spanish history have helped define American culture. For example, the 13th-century king of Spain, Alfonso X, also known as the Learned, may be unknown to the majority of Americans, but his work on the codification of Spanish law has greatly influenced the evolution of American law, particularly in the jurisdictions of the Southwest. For this contribution a statue of him stands in the rotunda of the Capitol in Washington, D.C. Likewise, the name Diego Rivera may be unfamiliar to most Americans, but this Mexican painter influenced many American artists whose paintings, commissioned during the Great Depression and the New Deal era of the 1930s, adorn the walls of government buildings throughout the United States. In recent years the contributions of Puerto Ricans, Mexicans, Mexican Americans (Chicanos), and Cubans in American cities such as Boston, Chicago, Los Angeles, Miami, Minneapolis, New York, and San Antonio have been enormous.

The importance of the Spanish language in this vast cultural complex cannot be overstated. Spanish, after all, is second only to English as the most widely spoken of Western languages within the United States as well as in the entire world. The popularity of the Spanish language in America has a long history.

In addition to Spanish exploration of the New World, the great Spanish literary tradition served as a vehicle for bringing the language and culture to America. Interest in Spanish literature in America began when English immigrants brought with them translations of Spanish masterpieces of the Golden Age. As early as 1683, private libraries in Philadelphia and Boston contained copies of the first picaresque novel, *Lazarillo de Tormes*, translations of Francisco de Quevedo's *Los Sueños*, and copies of the immortal epic of reality and illusion *Don Quixote*, by the great Spanish writer Miguel de Cervantes. It would not be surprising if Cotton Mather, the arch-Puritan, read *Don Quixote* in its original Spanish, if only to enrich his vocabulary in preparation for his writing *La fe del cristiano en 24 artículos de la Institución de Cristo, enviada a los españoles para que abran sus ojos* (The Christian's Faith in 24 Articles of the Institution of Christ, Sent to the Spaniards to Open Their Eyes), published in Boston in 1699.

Over the years, Spanish authors and their works have had a vast influence on American literature—from Washington Irving, John Steinbeck, and Ernest Hemingway in the novel to Henry Wadsworth Longfellow and Archibald MacLeish in poetry. Such important American writers as James Fenimore Cooper, Edgar Allan Poe, Walt Whitman, Mark Twain, and Herman Melville all owe a sizable debt to the Spanish literary tradition. Some writers, such as Willa Cather and Maxwell Anderson, who explored Spanish themes they came into contact with in the American Southwest and Mexico, were influenced less directly but no less profoundly.

Important contributions to a knowledge of Spanish culture in the United States were also made by many lesser known individuals—teachers, publishers, historians, entrepreneurs, and others—with a love for Spanish culture. One of the most significant of these contributions was made by Abiel Smith, a Harvard College graduate of the class of 1764, when he bequeathed stock worth $20,000 to Harvard for the support of a professor of French and Spanish. By 1819 this endowment had produced enough income to appoint a professor, and the philologist and humanist George Ticknor became the first holder of the Abiel

Smith Chair, which was the very first endowed Chair at Harvard University. Other illustrious holders of the Smith Chair would include the poets Henry Wadsworth Longfellow and James Russell Lowell.

A highly respected teacher and scholar, Ticknor was also a collector of Spanish books, and as such he made a very special contribution to America's knowledge of Spanish culture. He was instrumental in amassing for Harvard libraries one of the first and most impressive collections of Spanish books in the United States. He also had a valuable personal collection of Spanish books and manuscripts, which he bequeathed to the Boston Public Library.

With the creation of the Abiel Smith Chair, Spanish language and literature courses became part of the curriculum at Harvard, which also went on to become the first American university to offer graduate studies in Romance languages. Other colleges and universities throughout the United States gradually followed Harvard's example, and today Spanish language and culture may be studied at most American institutions of higher learning.

No discussion of the Spanish influence in the United States, however brief, would be complete without a mention of the Spanish influence on art. Important American artists such as John Singer Sargent, James A. M. Whistler, Thomas Eakins, and Mary Cassatt all explored Spanish subjects and experimented with Spanish techniques. Virtually every serious American artist living today has studied the work of the Spanish masters as well as the great 20th-century Spanish painters Salvador Dalí, Joan Miró, and Pablo Picasso.

The most pervasive Spanish influence in America, however, has probably been in music. Compositions such as Leonard Bernstein's *West Side Story*, the Latinization of William Shakespeare's *Romeo and Juliet* set in New York's Puerto Rican quarter, and Aaron Copland's *Salon Mexico* are two obvious examples. In general, one can hear the influence of Latin rhythms—from tango to mambo, from guaracha to salsa—in virtually every form of American music.

This series of biographies, which Chelsea House has published under the general title HISPANICS OF ACHIEVEMENT, constitutes further recognition of—and a renewed effort to bring forth to the consciousness of America's young people—the contributions that Hispanic people have made not only in the United States but throughout the civilized world. The men and women who are featured in this series have attained a high level of accomplishment in their respective fields of endeavor and have made a permanent mark on American society.

The title of this series must be understood in its broadest possible sense: The term *Hispanics* is intended to include Spaniards, Spanish Americans, and individuals from many countries whose language and culture have either direct or indirect Spanish origins. The names of many of the people included in this series will be immediately familiar; others will be less recognizable. All, however, have attained recognition within their own countries, and often their fame has transcended their borders.

The series HISPANICS OF ACHIEVEMENT thus addresses the attainments and struggles of Hispanic people in the United States and seeks to tell the stories of individuals whose personal and professional lives in some way reflect the larger Hispanic experience. These stories are exemplary of what human beings can accomplish, often against daunting odds and by extraordinary personal sacrifice, where there is conviction and determination. Fray Junípero Serra, the 18th-century Spanish Franciscan missionary, is one such individual. Although in very poor health, he devoted the last 15 years of his life to the foundation of missions throughout California—then a mostly unsettled expanse of land—in an effort to bring a better life to Native Americans through the cultivation of crafts and animal husbandry. An example from recent times, the Mexican-American labor leader Cesar Chavez has battled bitter opposition and made untold personal sacrifices in his effort to help poor agricultural workers who have been exploited for decades on farms throughout the Southwest.

The talent with which each one of these men and women may have been endowed required dedication and hard work to develop and become fully realized. Many of them have enjoyed rewards for their efforts during their own lifetime, whereas others have died poor and unrecognized. For some it took a long time to achieve their goals, for others success came at an early age, and for still others the struggle continues. All of them, however, stand out as people whose lives have made a difference, whose achievements we need to recognize today and should continue to honor in the future.

Octavio Paz

THE POWER OF
THE POET

If a thousand men were not to pay their tax-bills this year, that would not be a violent and bloody measure, as it would be to pay them, and enable the State to commit violence and shed innocent blood. ... If the tax-gatherer, or any other public officer, asks me, as one has done, 'But what shall I do?' my answer is, 'If you really wish to do anything, resign your office.'" Henry David Thoreau wrote these words in his stirring essay "Civil Disobedience," first published in Boston in 1849. For this 19th-century American writer, a person did not have a moral obligation to concern himself with political affairs. He or she *was* obliged, however, to disassociate himself from corrupt and bloody governments by not supporting them with money—either through taxes or by accepting their pay.

The issues for Thoreau were his opposition to slavery, at that time supported by the U.S. government, and an unjust war against a weaker power: the United States had attacked its southern neighbor, Mexico, and taken vast tracts of land. In the years to come, Thoreau's call for action was heard by many protest leaders throughout the world: both Mahatma Gandhi,

Octavio Paz, photographed in 1966, when he was Mexico's ambassador to India. Paz enjoyed a stimulating and productive life in India, but he resigned his post in 1968 as an act of political protest.

15

a leader in the fight for India's independence during the late 1940s, and the U.S. civil rights leader Martin Luther King, Jr., who led the struggle against racism during the 1950s and 1960s, read Thoreau and acknowledged their debt to him.

Over one hundred and twenty years after the appearance of Thoreau's essay, halfway around the globe from New England in New Delhi, India, a 54-year-old Mexican poet and diplomat was contemplating a personal response to his government's shedding of innocent blood. As news of a massacre in his hometown of Mexico City reached him in New Delhi, India, the nation that Gandhi had helped to free from foreign rule, Octavio Paz realized that his own time for action had arrived.

Between 1962 and 1968, Paz had served as the Mexican ambassador in New Delhi. His time in the East had been particularly fruitful. He had continued his study of Indian culture and had deepened his knowledge of Eastern civilizations. In his book *Pasión crítica* (Critical Passion), he had stated the importance that Hindu culture held for him and his wife, the artist Marie-José Tramini: "India taught Marie-José and me about the existence of a civilization distinct from our own. We learned not only to respect it but to love it. Over all, we learned to keep silent."

Paz's scope as a writer, however, encompassed more than even the Indian subcontinent, with its sprawling cities and multitude of gods, could provide. Now at the top of his literary form—in the 1960s many readers began to consider him Mexico's most distinguished living writer—Paz was a master of poetic technique and highly skilled at expressing his vision. The range of his work embraced the native cultures of Mexico, the European literary tradition (especially that of France and Spain), and, most recently, the cultures of Asia, which he had come to know through his various diplomatic posts. Paz savored the poetry of countries around the globe, and the reading of verse was for him a form of devotion. "I'm always reading poetry," he once remarked. "Like Christians saying their prayers every night, I try always, every day, to read a poem or a poetical text."

While in New Delhi, he found time to read and reread the works of favorite poets as well the religious works essential to Buddhism. Paz later told the Argentine writer Rita Gilbert that the most important event of his stay in India was not a cultural revelation but rather a personal one: "In India I met my wife, Marie-José. After being born, that's the most important thing that has happened to me."

In 1968, the Pazes were living a comfortable life in New Delhi. As the Mexican ambassador, Paz enjoyed a well-paid and highly respected position. He entertained dignitaries in the ambassador's official residence and dealt with the infrequent diplomatic problems that arose between the Indian and Mexican governments. He had been at the call of the Mexican foreign service for over 30 years—work that enabled him to

Mexican university students rally in front of Mexico City's Metropolitan Cathedral in the summer of 1968. Student protests were erupting all over the world at the time, but the conflict was especially severe in Mexico, where the students and the government had been clashing for the past 10 years.

support himself and, more important, gave him
enough free time to continue his work as a prolific
poet, critic, and essayist. He could not have asked for a
better situation.

But in October of that year, Paz received disturb-
ing news from his country. After a decade of conflict
between university students and the Mexican government—from the widespread protests over the U.S.-
backed invasion of Cuba at the Bay of Pigs in 1962 to
the student strikes in 1967 at the University of Guer-
rero that resulted in the expulsion of all suspected
leftists from the university—tensions were running
high between the state and the academic world.

In the summer of 1968, students were again
rebelling against the government, and Paz saw in these
demonstrations a reflection of his own hopes and
struggles as a youth growing up in Mexico City.
Indeed, protests were erupting throughout the world.
From Prague to Chile and from Belgrade to Rome,
student rebellions were commonplace, and sometimes
they turned violent. But the clash in Mexico City,
which would shatter Paz's faith in his own government, resulted in the greatest amount of blood spilled
that year.

In an attempt to quell the growing tension between the government and the university in Mexico
City, the city's chief of police ordered the detainment
of various university officials. But this measure only
angered the university's students. Student strikes were
called to achieve certain demands, including the
recognition of democratic liberties and the disbanding
of police forces now appearing on campuses in greater
numbers.

A general uprising ensued on the vast campus of
the Autonomous National University of Mexico,
known as UNAM, on the outskirts of Mexico City.
Festivals were commonplace that summer, with

painters, artists, and singers entertaining the crowds. As protests began to spill out onto the city streets, the army was called out—fully equipped with tanks, jeeps, and bazookas. The government was so concerned about the extent of the protests that it sent security forces onto the campus to keep order. The flag at UNAM was flown at half mast in mourning for the violation of the university's independence, an important principle in Latin America. On July 30, the university's rector made an impassioned speech to the students and professors:

> The University is first, and we will remain united to defend, both inside and outside of our home, the freedom to think, to gather, to express ourselves, and the most expensive liberty of all: Our autonomy! Long live UNAM! Long Live the Autonomous University!

The Mexican president at the time, Gustavo Díaz Ordaz, was a dour man with very little tolerance for opposition. He ordered severe repression of the student uprisings, and there was little opposition from his advisers. Beginning in the 1940s—and continuing into the 1990s—the governing party of Mexico was the Partido Revolucionario Institucional (Institutional Revolutionary party), or PRI. Although the PRI maintained its monopoly through democratic elections, intimidation and bribery were sometimes used to ensure election results. About the PRI, Paz would later write: "More than a political party in the traditional sense of the word, PRI is a gigantic bureaucracy, a machine of control and manipulation of the masses."

After months of bitter protests and government retaliation, events took a tragic turn. On October 2, a meeting was called by the National Council of Strikes, the student organization that orchestrated many of the protests that year. Approximately 10,000 students, concerned parents, and workers gathered at the Plaza

A student demonstrator is clubbed by a riot policeman in Mexico City in September 1968. In the face of growing unrest, Mexico's president, Gustavo Díaz Ordaz, ordered a crackdown that soon reached a tragic and bloody climax.

de las Tres Culturas in Tlatelelco, near the center of Mexico City. With the Summer Olympics soon to begin in Mexico City, government officials were anxious to quell the student uprising, which might focus international attention on the PRI's repressive political tactics. Five thousand soldiers were ordered to the scene. The Olympic Battalion, a paramilitary group specially trained to keep order during the upcoming Olympic Games, was also sent to the scene. The soldiers were equipped with tanks, jeeps, assault cars, machine guns, and automatic pistols. There were reports that some of the students were carrying guns.

The meeting opened at 5:30 P.M. The leaders of the protest announced that they were canceling a planned march but that they would begin a hunger strike the following week. At 6:10, a helicopter flew over the crowd and fired two green flares over the plaza—the signal for the armed forces to move in. Quickly the Olympic Battalion infiltrated the crowd. Many of them were dressed as civilians, except for a white glove or handkerchief worn over the left hand as a sign to other soldiers that the wearer was undercover. Amid a sudden eruption of gunshots, the special forces moved quickly into a nearby building and seized the strike leaders on the third floor.

The entire plaza was quickly surrounded. Marksmen came out from hiding on the roofs of nearby buildings, and as they opened fire upon the crowd, the Plaza de las Tres Culturas was drenched in blood. Although the official Mexican press reported that 32 people had been killed, eyewitnesses and foreign correspondents put the death toll far higher— at more than 300 unarmed persons. In the general chaos that followed the attack, at least 500 hundred students and workers were hurt, and 2,000 were arrested.

Upon learning of the massacre, Paz felt that he could not allow such a horrendous act to pass unnoticed. Though he had never shied away from tackling political and moral issues, Paz did not routinely make pronouncements on public affairs, in contrast to more overtly political poets such as Pablo Neruda. As the critic Emir Rodríguez Monegal pointed out, Paz "takes notes before speaking, answers questions with extreme caution, and then phrases and rephrases his words until they have the bite of his critical essays."

After Tlatelelco, Paz's response to his government's actions was swift and unmistakable. First, he resigned his ambassadorial post in protest. And although he had previously declined an invitation by the Olympic organizing committee to write a poem in celebration of the event, Paz now penned "México: olimpiada de 1968" (Mexico City: The 1968 Olympiad) to express his anger. He also wrote an essay entitled "Olympics and Tlatelelco," in which he reflected upon the deeper meanings of the October 2 outrage:

> The regime showed that it was neither willing nor able to examine its own conscience.... This mental and moral weakness led to the physical violence. Like those neurotics who retreat when confronted with new and difficult situations, who swing from fear to rage, who commit insensate acts in a regression to the instinctive behavior of infants or

animals, the government regressed to earlier periods in the history of Mexico.... Its resemblances to Mexico's past, especially to the Aztec world, are fascinating, frightening, and repellent.

Paz wrote articles and held interviews with newspapers and magazines from all over the world to bring attention to his government's brutal action. He noted the coincidence that the bloodshed had occurred at the site of an Aztec pyramid, where centuries earlier gruesome sacrifices had been performed. He angrily called for the institution of democratic reforms in Mexico, the only way he could see for his country to come to terms with its ideals and its failures. Paz was well aware of the power that these protests held, coming as they did from a former ambassador and an internationally known poet. Commenting on the writer's role in society, he later said: "The word of the writer is powerful because it comes from a position of nonpower. He does not speak from the National Palace, the popular tribune, or the offices of the Central Committee: He speaks from his room."

Paz took advantage of this unique power for many years after the massacre at Tlatelelco. In 1984, he collected the articles he had written in defense of the democratic process and published them in two volumes, *El ogro filantrópico* (The Philanthropic Ogre) and *Tiempo nublado* (Cloudy Weather). These books alienated many of those on the political left who had applauded Paz for his 1968 protest: in his essays Paz not only attacked right-wing repression but also trained his fire on the left-wing govenments of Cuba, Nicaragua, and the Soviet Union, all of which denied their citizens many democratic freedoms. Though they aroused criticism, the essays also confirmed Paz's stature as an independent thinker and a champion of artistic and political liberty.

In 1968, the Mexican government reacted angrily to Paz's criticisms, accusing him of disloyalty to his

Heavily armed troops confront protestors in Mexico City in 1968. When soldiers massacred more than 300 civilians in the Plaza de las Tres Culturas on October 2, Paz lashed out at the government, calling its "frightening and repellent" actions a throwback to the days of gruesome Aztec sacrifices.

country. He was one of many writers and intellectuals over whom the government declared a blackout of information. Although his books were still available, no mention of his work, including reviews or interviews, would be accepted by the mainstream press or media. (However, as the well-known novelist Carlos Fuentes noted in a letter to Paz, the blackout only served to increase the popularity of the writers who were on it; Paz's and Fuentes's books began to sell better than ever in Mexico.) It would not be until many years later, after he returned to Mexico City and gained international awards, including the Nobel Prize for literature, that his country would accept him as its own—the greatest living Latin American poet.

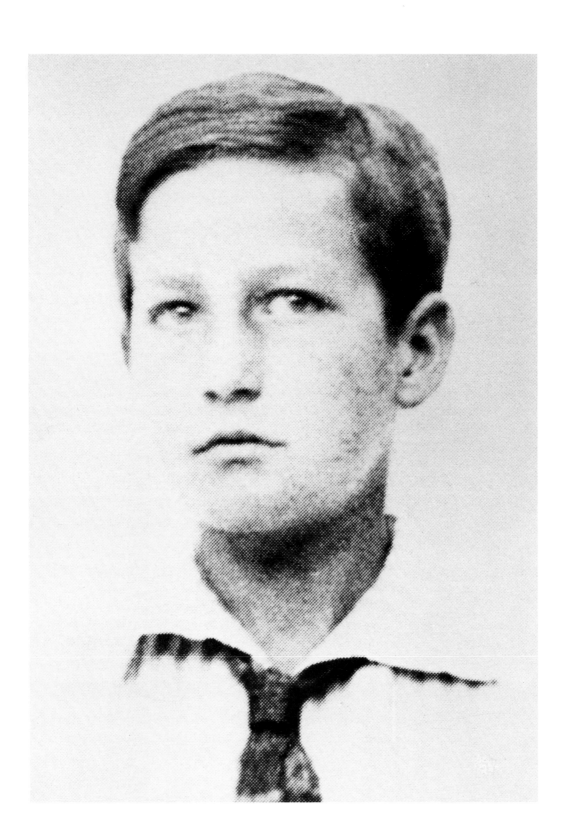

MEXICO AND MIXCOAC

On April 1, 1914, an article appeared in the Mexico City newspaper *La Patria* (The Homeland):

> With great joy, [in her home at number 14 Venecia, in the Colonia Juárez] Doña Josefina Lozano, the wife of the lawyer Octavio Paz Solórzano, the son of our director, had her first childbirth this morning, bringing to the light a healthy young boy. We warmly welcome him, and we hope he will be good for the family and for the country, we count on him as a new defender of our autonomy.

The child, Octavio Paz Lozano, had been born in Mexico City on March 31, 1914. His grandfather, Ireneo Paz Flores, was the director of *La Patria* at the time, and his father was deeply involved in the political changes going on in the country. *La Patria*, like almost every newspaper in Mexico, was deeply concerned for the future of the country. The nation was in the midst of a 10-year civil war, a struggle in which the infant's father would play an integral role.

Octavio Paz Solórzano was truly Mexican. His family was *mestizo*, of both Spanish and Indian descent, and they had come to Mexico City from the state of Jalisco. Jalisco, home of wide-brimmed

Octavio Paz at the age of 10. Born in the midst of a civil war, young Octavio inherited a family tradition of literary excellence and political commitment.

25

sombreros, *charreados* (Mexican rodeos), and mariachi music, is located high in the Sierra Madre and is often considered to be the "most Mexican" state. Octavio Paz Solórzano, following in the footsteps of his father, Ireneo Paz, was both a political activist and a writer.

In the late 19th century and on into the early years of the 20th century, Ireneo Paz had been a good friend to Porfirio Díaz, the dictator whose harsh methods helped to bring about the Mexican Revolution and his own downfall at the hands of the rebels. Díaz had not only overseen the virtual enslavement of Mexico's native peoples to criollo landowners (those of pure Spanish descent, who considered themselves a higher caste than natives or those of mixed ancestry); he had

Mexican president Porfirio Díaz (1830–1915), whose repressive policies helped bring about the Mexican Revolution in the early 20th century. Although Ireneo Paz, Octavio's grandfather, was a friend of Díaz's, he embraced the democratic principles that Octavio was to champion throughout his adult life.

also intensified Mexico's relationship with the United States—further angering the revolutionaries, who fervently opposed foreign influence in their country.

Despite Ireneo Paz's connection with Díaz, he maintained that he was a liberal man.

Octavio Paz Solórzano was a staunch proponent of democratic freedoms, such as the liberty to think as one wished and the freedom of the press. Since his student days, he had fought long and hard for these rights. When the revolution began, he quickly sided with the revolutionaries. Porfirio Díaz was successfully overthrown in 1911, and in the ensuing turmoil, Octavio Paz Solórzano found himself siding with one of the most controversial of the Mexican revolutionaries: Emiliano Zapata.

The young lawyer saw in Zapata a strength of character and a dedication to the poor that he found lacking in other factions vying for power in Mexico. He joined with Zapata and, through his legal skills, worked to improve the position of his leader. Paz Solórzano continued to struggle for agrarian reform after the revolution, helping to obtain land for the peasants who had been working for large landowners for ages.

Paz Solórzano had completed his legal studies in November 1911, only a few years before he joined up with Zapata. On December 29 of that year, he married Josefina Lozano, a beautiful woman whom he had met on occasion at fiestas around Mexico City. Two months after their marriage, the couple took their honeymoon at Esenda de Todos Santos, in Baja California. The small town by the sea was a perfect setting for the newlyweds. Josefina, petite and slender, spent much of her vacation enjoying the sea breeze and basking in the sun. Octavio leisurely worked on some articles for his father's paper and went over his legal work. After returning to Mexico City, the couple

Josefina Lozano Paz, Octavio's mother, as a young woman. Of pure Spanish descent, Josefina was not an intellectual like her husband, but she provided her son with a warm and loving home life.

would remember this time as among the most pleasant and tranquil days of their lives.

Josefina Lozano Paz was from a criollo family. Her father, Francisco Lozano, was a wine merchant, and her mother, Concepción O. de Lozano, took care of the family's home. Both sides of Josefina Lozano's family had come from the southern Spanish province of Andalusia, known for its spirited horses and its fighting bulls.

Octavio's family life was warm and sheltering. But it proved no match for the revolution now raging in the streets of Mexico, and the family, economically devastated, retreated from Mexico City. The Pazes moved to a rundown house in Mixcoac, on the outskirts of the city. Their house was owned by Octavio's grandfather, and for years to come it harbored Octavio, his parents, and an eccentric aunt.

Mixcoac was a small village that could trace its origins back to the days before Columbus sailed to the New World. Its name derived from the god Mixcoatl, the Cloud Serpent that represented the Milky Way in native mythology. The village was drenched in Mexican history, with monuments to the country's past, before and after the Spanish arrived, standing in the form of a pre-Columbian pyramid and a 16th-century colonial church. Before the revolution, the Mexican middle class had used Mixcoac as a summer retreat, and the Pazes' house—once merely Ireneo Paz's summer home—was surrounded by pleasant

The Mexican revolutionary leader Emiliano Zapata (1879–1919) was a dynamic and controversial figure who championed the rights of Mexico's peasants. When Octavio Paz's father was sent to Los Angeles as Zapata's representative, young Octavio got his first taste of North American life.

18th- and 19th-century homes. Although young Octavio's intellectual and social heritage was rich—his house was filled with the portraits and mementos of dead ancestors—his family had little money. Paz recalled that the entire house was in a state of decay: his own bedroom had crumbling walls that were covered with cloth sheets.

When Octavio was about six years old, his mother took him to the United States. Octavio's father had been sent to Los Angeles as an emissary for Zapata. Money was tight in the small apartment that the three of them shared in Los Angeles's Mexican barrio, or ghetto. Young Octavio faced a big challenge when his parents enrolled him in kindergarten that year. On the first day of school, the boy was terrified. Although he tried to argue his parents out of sending him, they eventually won out, and Octavio reluctantly went off to school.

During lunch on that first day, the shy foreign student realized that he needed a spoon but did not know how to ask for one in English. All he could think of was the Spanish word—*cuchara*. When he tried to make himself understood, his American classmates began to tease him. Octavio lost his temper, and a fight broke out in the lunchroom. From that day on, the other students called him Cuchara. Octavio did not enjoy this nickname. "For me it was an insult," he later said, "because it reminded me of my ignorance."

In less than a year, the Paz family returned to its home in Mixcoac. But even in his native country, Octavio had problems. Once again he was teased for being different. To his Mexican companions, the new boy from up north was now an outsider. Octavio discovered that he was a foreigner even in his own country. Once again, he tried to solve his problems with his fists.

Rebel troops board a train at Veracruz during the Mexican Revolution, which raged from 1901 to 1911. The Paz family, financially ruined by the turmoil surrounding the revolution, had to move from Mexico City to the humble village of Mixcoac; there, young Octavio was immersed in the myths and history of Mexico.

But in his grandfather's house, the child was surrounded by an atmosphere that favored reflection and insight—qualities that would distinguish Paz throughout his later years. Ireneo Paz treasured the great literary works of Europe, and it was in his grandfather's cozy, well-stocked library that Octavio found many classics of Latin, Greek, Spanish, and French literature. With the encouragement of his aunt, Octavio also began to explore the wealth of books on French art and literature, spawning an interest in French culture that would continue throughout his life.

In contrast to those reflective, quiet hours at home, there were great street festivals in the village throughout the year, with fireworks and entertainment for people of all ages. In Mixcoac, as throughout Mexico, religious fiestas were celebrated with great fervor, as well as with toys, fruits, candies, costumes, and lots of alcohol. Paz later wrote about these fiestas, which continue to thrive in Mexico, in his book *El laberinto de la soledad* (The Labyrinth of Solitude):

Our calendar is crowded with fiestas. There are certain days when the whole country, from the most remote villages to the largest cities, prays, shouts, feasts, gets drunk and kills, in honor of the Virgin of Guadalupe [the patron saint of Mexico] or Benito Juárez [a former president]. . . . During the days before and after the twelfth of December, time comes to a full stop, and instead of pushing us toward a deceptive tomorrow that is always beyond our reach, offers a complete and perfect today of dancing and revelry, of communion with the most ancient and secret Mexico.

Octavio Paz in 1924, with his aunt, a cousin, and his grandfather. The death of Ireneo Paz at the age of 89 during the same year severed young Octavio's deepest tie to his native country.

Yet these religious holidays and indeed his whole Catholic education were beginning to trouble the young boy. Paz later described to Rita Gilbert his religious doubts, initiated in part by his reading of the 18th-century French writer Voltaire. "As a boy, because of my aunt and my mother, I went to a French school kept by Marist fathers, and like all boys I went through a crisis of religious enthusiasm. I was very anxious to find out if my grandfather, who wasn't a believer but whom I considered to be one of the best men in the world, would be saved or not. For him to be condemned to hell seemed to me atrocious."

In 1924, when Octavio was 10 years old, his grandfather Ireneo Paz died, an event Paz later recalled in his poem "Elegía interrumpida" (Interrupted Elegy). After this loss, the house in Mixcoac must have felt empty to the young boy. As he grew older, Octavio would spend more and more time in Mexico City. But eventually even Mexico City would seem too restricting to the young man, and he would begin to explore cities and countries throughout the world. Yet the memory of the gentle days of his childhood would never leave him. In "Estrofas para un jardín imaginado" (Verses for an Imagined Garden), Paz recalled Mixcoac as it once was, the small town of his childhood. The poem also expressed his early discovery of inspiration and of poetry itself.

> One afternoon, as I left running from primary school, I stopped suddenly, I felt myself to be in the center of the world. I raised my eyes and saw, between the clouds, an open blue sky, indecipherable, infinite. I didn't know what to say: I understood enthusiasm and, perhaps, poetry.

That powerful intuition was to shape the course of his adult life.

THE ACT OF WORDS

Octavio Paz entered the National Preparatory School in San Ildefonso when he was 16. The school had been built in the 17th century and contained murals by the Mexican painter José Clemente Orozco as well as the first mural ever painted by the controversial Mexican artist Diego Rivera. It was recognized as one of the finest schools in the country.

When Paz enrolled, the school was a hotbed of political activity. The man who had sponsored Rivera's paintings in the National Preparatory had been the minister of education, José Vasconcelos. Both philosopher and educational reformist, Vasconcelos had been responsible for the establishment of over 2,000 rural schools throughout Mexico. He had also inspired the students themselves to demand educational and political reforms. When a student was shot down in the city during one of the protests, the student movement quickly became more unified and impassioned. Paz joined the Student Union for Workers and Peasants. He and his friends gathered at night, walking through the streets of Mexico City, discussing literature and philosophy and sometimes boisterously arguing politics and their plans for social change.

Although he took part in the student strikes that disrupted classes throughout that year, Paz continued

Octavio Paz at the age of 16, when he entered the National Preparatory School. At this school, founded by an educational pioneer, Paz discovered modern literature and deepened his commitment to social justice.

his studies whenever possible, and it was at the National Preparatory that he was first introduced to
modern writers; his grandfather's library, excellent
though it was, ended at the beginning of the 20th
century. At school, Paz was captivated by the writings
of the French novelist Marcel Proust as well as the
revolutionary Spanish poets of the Generation of
1927, such as Federico García Lorca. The poems of the
Argentine Jorge Luis Borges and, perhaps most important of all, the Chilean Pablo Neruda were a
revelation for the adolescent.

Amid the "dreams and deliriums of youth," Paz
walked the streets of Mixcoac and Mexico City, ab-
sorbing everything that he saw—echoing in many
ways the student life-style that Neruda himself had
revealed in works such as *Veinte poemas de amor y una
canción desesperada* (Twenty Love Poems and a Song of
Despair) and *Crepusculario* (Twilight Book). More
than 50 years later, Paz recalled his adolescence in
"1930: vistas fijas" (1930: Scenic Views):

*The great Spanish poet
Federico García Lorca
(1898–1936) was one of
the authors Paz most
admired during his school
days. By his second year at
the National Preparatory,
Paz began a literary review,*
Barandal, *in which he
published his first poems.*

Who or what guided me? I was not searching for anything or anyone, I was searching for everything, searching for everyone:

the vegetation of blue cupolas and the white bell-towers, walls the color of dried blood, architectures:

a banquet of forms, a petrified dance under the clouds that make and unmake and never stop making themselves, always in transit toward their future forms,

ocher stones tattooed by an angry star, stones washed by the water of the moon. . .

streets that never ended, streets walked as one reads a book or travels over a body . . .

With two generations of politically active Pazes preceding him, it should not have come as a surprise when Octavio threw himself into political activity at such an early age. Through the Student Union, he began teaching night classes for workers who gathered from around the city. Sometimes these classes turned into political meetings.

Yet Paz's adolescence was dedicated to much more than social causes. A young poet was emerging, with a passionate interest in language and words. In "Nocturno de San Ildefonso" (San Ildefonso Nocturne), written decades later, Paz recaptured the essence of his youthful calling.

Between seeing and making,
                              contemplation or action,
I chose the act of words:
                              to make them, to inhabit them,
to give eyes to the language.

At the beginning of his second year at National Preparatory, Paz began a small literary review, *Barandal* (Balustrade), along with three friends—Rafael López Malo, Arnulfo Martínez Lavalle, and Salvador Toscano. It was here that he published his first poems. Of all his juvenile work, however, Paz would later only recognize a few poetic attempts as being worthy of attention. (Most of his early poems as they appear in his collection *Libertad bajo palabra* (Liberty on Parole) are actually recreations of these earlier works. Paz constantly revises and re-revises his poetry and his other writings.)

Through *Barandal* the students were given a chance to meet some of Mexico's most respected poets. In each issue, the young writers solicited works from those poets they most admired—Carlos Pellicer, Salvador Novo, and Xavier Villaurrutia, who later became a close friend of Paz's. The adolescent loyally read the literary magazine *Contemporáneos* (Contemporaries), in which many of these poets published their work. Through this magazine, Paz was also introduced to modern poetry from outside the Spanish-speaking world. In one issue, a translation of T. S. Eliot's *The Waste Land* especially affected the young writer.

The poems that made up Paz's first book, *Luna Silvestre* (Rustic Moon), published in 1933, are now almost completely forgotten. Paz's poetry at this time was intimate in nature; he mostly wrote sonnets and nocturnes. In a conversation with the writer Julián Ríos in 1973, Paz recalled the reaction of Rafael Alberti, a Spanish poet who was also a dedicated Communist, to this early work: "And when I showed my poetry to Alberti he told me: 'well, this isn't social poetry . . . this isn't revolutionary poetry in the political sense'—Alberti said—'but Octavio is the only revolutionary poet among you, because he is the only one who has made an attempt to transform the language.' And these words of Alberti made a great impression on me."

Paz finished his schooling at the National Preparatory in 1932. His family had decided that he should pursue a legal career, and he went on to study at the Escuela de Derecho (law school) in Mexico City. At this time he also began to pursue his lifelong

The Metropolitan Cathedral in Mexico City. After his father died in a train accident in 1934, Paz began to withdraw from his formerly active social life. He began to spend time alone and found the familiar surroundings of Mexico City rather confining.

passion for literary criticism. He not only wrote about writers whom he had read for years, such as Proust, but also about German, English and French poets. He also wrote essays about the leading Latin American poets, including Carlos Pellicer, Jorge Luis Borges, Pablo Neruda, and Cesar Vallejo. Some of these essays appeared in Paz's second literary magazine, *Cuadernos del Valle de Mexico* (Notebooks of the Valley of Mexico), which he began in 1933.

In 1934, when Paz was 20 years old, a tragedy struck his family. His father was killed in a train accident, perhaps due to heavy drinking. It was not until many years later that Paz could write about the pain that this event had caused him as a young man.

After his father's death, Paz became more reflective and withdrawn. Mexico began to feel small, provincial, removed from the outside world. His habit of writing poetry late at night, in the silence and solitude of his room, only increased his sense of isolation. He began to question his desire to become a lawyer. As soon as Paz was given the opportunity, he would explore new regions and cultures: from the Yucatán Peninsula to the literary hot spot of the world, Paris, France.

In January 1937, a small book of Paz's poetry, *Raíz del hombre* (Root of Man), was released. Although only a few of the poems from this work survived Paz's later self-editing, some of the poet's lifelong poetic concerns emerge in this work. The concrete and sensuous nature of his imagery, for example, wedded to philosophical and mystical concerns, is clearly evident:

> In fearless white spirals
> we approach our origins and roots
> going backwards in age, dreams, time:
>
> vegetation calls us
> the stone remembers us
> and the sedentary root
> of the tree grows from our dust.

Among those impressed with Paz's youthful work was the Mexican poet Jorge Cuesta. He invited Paz to a dinner with many of the established poets of Mexico City—initiating him into the realm of the Contemporáneos (Contemporaries), a group of poets who were centered around the magazine of the same name, published between 1928 and 1931. Although most of the Contemporáneos lived in Mexico City, Paz noticed that their poetry lacked the basic element of the city—people. "In Pellicer there are mountains, rivers, trees, ruins; there are also stereotyped heroes

The Argentine writer Jorge Luis Borges (1899–1986) had a distinct influence on the young Paz. Borges's fascination with other cultures, particularly those of Asia, was also a hallmark of Paz's own literary career.

and villains but there aren't people. . . . In the poems of Gorostiza, Villaurrutia and Ortiz de Montellano there isn't anyone: everyone and everything has turned into reflections, specters."

Paz's differences with these poets would later help him to form his own style and point of view. But as a youth, he was more than thrilled to feel that he might belong in the company of such distinguished writers.

CEREMONY IN THE CATACOMBS

Octavio Paz at the age of 18, photographed during a trip to southern Mexico. At this time he was still planning to be a lawyer; but four years later, he abandoned his studies in order to take a teaching job in the remote Yucatán Peninsula.

At the age of 22, Paz decided to abandon his law studies and leave his home in Mexico City. Although he had just begun to establish himself with the poets of Mexico City, he could not resist the impulse to see other parts of Mexico and the world. When an opportunity arose for him to teach the children of peasants and laborers in the small city of Mérida on the Yucatán Peninsula, he quickly took it. Although Paz stayed in this hot tropical region of Mexico for only four months, he quickly realized how little he knew about his own country. Here in the tropics he was not only a man from the mountains—more important, he was a city dweller.

Yet his situation as a lone outsider did not last for long. He soon formed a Pro-Democracy Committee for Spain, in support of the Republic in the Spanish Civil War, which broke out in 1936. He also wrote articles on life in the Yucatán. His "Notes" were published in the Mexico City magazine *El Nacional* (The National).

In these articles, Paz discovered a symbol for the life of the region—henequen, a durable fiber derived from the agave plant and used primarily to manufacture twine. In the Yucatán at this time there were still large plantations on which workers toiled for a meager wage, gathering the agave leaves and weaving the twine that was to be sold abroad. Paz's political awareness grew as he witnessed the injustices suffered by the workers.

While he was in Mérida, Paz received an invitation from the Chilean poet Pablo Neruda (to whom the young poet had sent a copy of *Raíz del hombre*), Rafael Alberti, and others, asking him to take part in the Second International Congress of Anti-Fascist Writers for the Defense of Culture. The congress was designed to lend support to the Loyalists of Republican Spain, who were defending the democratic government against the right-wing forces led by Francisco Franco. Although most of the Mexican writers and artists who attended the congress were members of the Communist party and of the League of Revolutionary Artists and Writers (LEAR), Paz himself was a member of neither. As he later explained to Julián Ríos, "I had had difficulties with a group of writers and painters who obediently followed the directives of the Communist Party." But Paz *was* a staunch supporter of the Spanish Republic, as was the Mexican government itself—along with the Soviet Union, Mexico was the only country to give military support to the Republic. Paz quickly accepted Neruda's invitation.

Before he departed for Spain, Paz married Elena Garro in Mexico City. At the time, Paz was 23, and Garro was just about to turn 18. The marriage did not last; the couple divorced several years later, after they had had a child, Helena. After the breakup, Garro went on to write a novel, *Los recuerdos de porvenir* (Memories of the Future), and to work as a journalist and a film director.

After making stops in the United States and Canada, the newlyweds sailed to Europe and then took a train from Le Havre, France, to Paris. Not knowing a soul in the city, Paz was overjoyed to hear someone bellowing, "Octavio Paz! Octavio Paz!" throughout the station. A tall, smiling man approached him, remarked on his youth, and embraced him. Paz had at last met one of the most remarkable poets of his age—Pablo Neruda.

A few days later, Paz and Neruda joined a large number of writers on a train to Spain, including the French novelist André Malraux and the English poet Stephen Spender. Writers from around the world were making the same journey to meet with their Spanish counterparts in Madrid and Valencia. José Bergamín, Antonio Machado, Rafael Alberti, and

The Chilean poet Pablo Neruda, photographed when he was in his teens. After Paz sent Neruda a book of poems, the Chilean extended an invitation for Paz to join a group of writers supporting the Loyalists in the Spanish Civil War.

The French novelist and archaeologist André Malraux was one of the writers Paz met during his trip to Spain in 1937. Paz's experiences at the Spanish front imbued him with a fervent belief in justice and liberty.

Miguel Hernández were among the illustrious Spanish poets that would greet the international delegation.

Paz was intrigued by Spain. He was, of course, aware of the debt that Mexican writers owed to the Spanish literary tradition, but traveling through the countryside, he saw how much the entire country of Mexico was a reflection of Spain; the architecture, the people, even the Spanish landscape seemed to have given birth to his own country. When he arrived at the congress, Paz met poets and writers who had fought side by side with the soldiers and working people of the Republic. For a while, he contemplated joining the Republican army.

Despite the differences that Paz had with many of the Communist poets at the meeting, he was deeply affected by the concept of a new society, a new humanity, in Republican Spain. Years later, while contemplating Mexico in *El laberinto de la soledad*, he would recall his vision:

> I remember that in Spain during the civil war I had a revelation of "the other man" and of another kind of solitude: not closed, not mechanical, but open to the transcendent. No doubt the nearness of death and the brotherhood of men-at-arms, at whatever time and in whatever country, always produce an atmosphere favorable to the extraordinary, to all that rises above the human condition and breaks the circle of solitude that surrounds each one of us. But in those faces—obtuse and obstinate, gross and brutal, like those the great Spanish painters, without the least touch of complacency and with an almost flesh and blood realism, have left us—there was something like a desperate hopefulness, something very concrete and at the same time universal. Since then I have never seen the same expression on any face.

The desperate fury of the war accelerated Paz's enthusiasm for militant poetry. Although he never did join the army, his poetry was filled with a fervor and dedication, if not to the Republic itself, at least to its highly charged ideals. In the early months of 1937, when the Fascist forces had surrounded the Republican stronghold in Madrid, Paz wrote "¡No pasarán!" (They Will Not Pass!), a poem that impressed many of his fellow writers in both Spain and Mexico. Nonetheless, Paz did not include the poem in any of his subsequent collections. Indeed, he later decided to abandon much of the verse that he wrote during his stay in Spain, perhaps because he felt that the immediacy of his words would be lost on future generations. Those poems that did survive the poet's self-editing, such as "Elegía a un joven muerto en el frente" (Elegy to a Young Man Killed at the Front), were altered to lessen the political nature of the verse.

Paz later recalled visiting a battlefield in Madrid with the Stephen Spender. Huddled in a building with a group of Loyalists, the two poets were separated from Nationalist soldiers only by a thin wall. Paz recalled, "We could hear the soldiers on the other side talking. It was a strange feeling: those people facing me—I couldn't see them but only hear their voices—were my enemies. But they had human voices, like my own. They were like me." This revelation led the poet to realize that all warfare was absurd and that one should acknowledge one's enemy, if not as a friend, at least as a fellow human.

Paz was in no hurry to go back home after the congress. Because this was his first trip to Europe, he decided to spend some time in France, which he had only briefly visited a few months earlier. In Paris, Paz was reunited with some of the writers whom he had met in Spain. Through the Cuban writer Alejo Carpentier, Paz was invited to a party thrown by the

Spanish Nationalist troops fire upon Loyalist troops outside Madrid in 1936. Though Paz avidly supported the Loyalist cause in Spain, he recognized that the Nationalist soldiers were also human beings deserving of compassion.

The boulevard Montmartre, in the heart of Paris's Left Bank. Traveling to the French capital after his visit to Spain, Paz was introduced to the surrealist movement. Surrealism, with its emphasis on the freedom of the imagination, became one of Paz's major enthusiasms.

French poet Robert Desnos. Although he was intimidated by the other guests—many of them were famous artists and writers—the contacts that Paz made at the party would help spur his interest in the artistic and literary trend then raging through Europe—surrealism.

Surrealism was a cultural movement that celebrated chance and spontaneity. Surrealist artists, and their audiences, were seeking liberation from the weight of the past and from the authority of academies and professors. The poets, for example, asserted that a poem should be written without any conscious thought: instead, the poet should allow ideas and images to pour forth in a process called automatic writing. As a result, striking combinations would often emerge, in which ideas, sensations, memories, and emotions would combine and clash. For painters, careful techniques developed over hundreds of years could be ignored: as Paz wrote of the Catalan artist Joan Miró, surrealism offered him the chance to paint "like a child five thousand years old."

The surrealists themselves believed that their movement reached far beyond the cultural sphere. Surrealist thinkers such as André Breton stated that dreams were superior to anything people experienced when awake, and they hoped for a future when the two realms of existence would unite to form an "absolute reality." In a 1925 surrealist manifesto claims such as these appear:

> Surrealism is not a new means of expression, nor a simpler one, nor even a metaphysic of poetry. It is a means of total liberation of the mind and of everything resembling it.
>
> We lay no claim to changing men's errors but we intend to show them the fragility of their thoughts, and on what shaky foundations, what hollow ground, they have built their shaking houses.
>
> We are specialists in Revolt. There is no means of action we are not capable of using if need arises.

For the young Mexican, such revolutionary ideas were liberating for both his poetry and his life.

After six months in Europe, Paz and Garro returned to Mexico City. Soon after their return, the poet Xavier Villaurrutia invited Paz to join him and other members of his literary circle at the Café Paris on Cinco de Mayo in the heart of Mexico City. Paz was thrilled to join these poets, outcasts all of them, in their pursuit of modern literature, or as Paz later referred to their poetic calling: "a ceremony in the catacombs." Each weekday between three and four in the afternoon they would gather, drink too much coffee, smoke too many cigarettes, discuss literature, and take jovial gibes at one another.

With a number of these poets, Paz founded the literary review *Taller* (Workshop) in 1938. Patterned after a magazine Paz had seen in Spain, *Taller* presented

Early issues of Taller, *the literary journal Paz helped to found upon his return to Mexico in 1938. Under the regime of President Lázaro Cárdenas, Mexico City became a refuge for European intellectuals who shared many of Paz's ideas about poetry and the visual arts.*

a fresh vision in Mexico. Although it supported social and political causes, contributions on art and literature were by no means restricted to a single viewpoint. The imagination was given free reign.

Taller was released at the right time. Under the leadership of General Lázaro Cárdenas, Mexico had become a magnet for European intellectuals fleeing the growing political savagery of their own continent. Paz later wrote of the progressive Mexican president: "Cárdenas was the only chief of state who gave asylum to [the deposed Soviet leader] Leon Trotsky. While he was in power, we had the sensation, strange over all, that we were governed by a man, a being like us." Mexican presidents were usually stern, strong-armed men. But under Cárdenas, a leader much loved throughout the country, Mexico was slowly opened to foreigners seeking political asylum. Besides accepting Trotsky, Mexico soon attracted a wide array of European thinkers and artists.

With the influx of the Europeans, Mexico City slowly began to shed its reputation as an intellectual backwater. But perhaps as the country gained in intellectual vigor, it lost the innocence and optimism that had often characterized the New World. For along with the misplaced Europeans came the bitter

memories of upheaval, war, and persecution, the sad-
ness of modern life, the loss of family and home, the
sense of alienation.

Some of the Spanish writers whom Paz had met
in Spain, such as Luis Cernuda and Juan Gil-Albert,
also moved to Mexico. Back in their home country,
the Republic was giving way before Franco's on-
slaught—the war was over by March 1939—and they
had fled for their lives. Paz's reputation in Mexico City
began to grow as a result of his association with the
expatriate writers and through his contributions to
Taller and another publication that he helped found, *El
Hijo Pródigo* (The Prodigal Son).

Paz continued to meet with his friend Villaurrutia
at the Café Paris, and the two began to discuss and
later to collaborate on two projects: *El Hijo Pródigo*
and *Laurel*, which grew out of an idea Paz's father had
had for an anthology of poetry in the Spanish language. Paz began to write his essays on art in this
period, beginning with "Isla de gracia" (Island of
Grace), a 1939 piece about art on the Greek island of
Crete. Even in these early essays, his emphasis on the
artistic vision—the freedom to express a personal,
unified view of the world—appears. All of the
magazines that Paz would later found or direct would
maintain this emphasis on the liberty of the imagination.

Along with the Spanish poets Emilio Prados and
Juan Gil-Albert, Paz and Villaurrutia gathered a large
body of work for *Laurel*. At the last minute, over the
objections of Paz and Gil-Albert, they themselves and
some other of the younger poets were omitted from
the work. Paz later admitted that he had been mistaken in objecting: at that time the poets of his generation had not yet earned their place in such an
anthology.

During the late 1930s, Paz and his fellow poets often gathered at the Café Paris on Mexico City's Cinco de Mayo, pictured below. Paz, who valued intellectual independence, became increasingly estranged from writers who insisted on following the dictates of the Communist party.

Despite all of Paz's literary work, he still had to hold a regular job in order to pay his bills. Among the variety of odd jobs that he held at this time, one of the most unusual involved counting old Mexican pesos before they were burned in a furnace in Mexico's Central Bank. Indeed, most of the poets who called themselves the Contemporáneos worked as functionaries in the Mexican government. In his long essay on Xavier Villaurrutia, Paz later explained why Mexican writers were so often attracted to the government for work: "For us the prestige of the State is immense. . . . In our value system, wealth and knowledge come after power. Mexican children dream of becoming presidents, not bankers."

At this time Paz met the exiled Soviet writer Victor Serge. Serge opened his eyes to the realities of life in the Soviet Union, whose government was becoming more and more oppressive under the control of Premier Joseph Stalin. Serge and other revolutionaries, who supported the more open policies of the deposed leader Leon Trotsky, were being imprisoned or expelled by Stalin, who ultimately executed millions of people he suspected of disloyalty.

Paz could thus hardly share the view of Communist writers who painted a rosy future for the Soviet Union, but he still tried to find a common position with them. This was a difficult task, because most Communists insisted that there was no middle ground: either one supported the Soviet Union, or one was an enemy of the revolution that was promising a new life for the world's workers. Unfortunately, Paz's friendship with Pablo Neruda could not withstand the strain of their differences, as Paz later disclosed in an interview with the American scholar Alfred MacAdam: "When [Neruda] came to Mexico, I saw him very often, but there were difficulties. First, there was a personal problem. Neruda was very generous, but also very domineering. Perhaps I was too rebellious and jealous of my own independence. He loved to be surrounded by a kind of court made up of people who loved him—sometimes these would be intelligent people but often they were mediocre. The second problem was politics. He became more and more Stalinist, while I became less and less enchanted with Stalin. Finally we fought—almost physically—and stopped speaking to each other." It would be decades before the two poets would see each other again.

Such clashes did not cause Paz to reverse his position on the freedom of the artist. He continued to argue, then and ever afterward, that all revolutionary governments—those that claim to fight for the good of humanity—must give their artists and writers total freedom. (More often than not, ironically, those governments have tried to control all forms of expression in the name of social progress.) Yet his growing political isolation in Mexico caused him to consider going into a self-imposed exile. Paz's poetry at this time reveals a degree of hopelessness and desolation. In "Noche de resurrecciones" (Night of the Resurrections), he lingers on images of pain:

> You hurt, cruel sweetness, blind nocturnal body
> of my uprooted blood; you hurt, painful branch,
> fallen among the forms, into the bowels of the world.

In 1942, Paz applied for a Guggenheim Fellowship to study in the United States, and he was soon pleased to receive it. He now had a convenient escape route from the oppressive atmosphere of Mexico City. The vast spaces of the United States beckoned him to the north.

ENTRE LO QUE VEO Y DIGO . . .

A Roman Jakobson

1

Entre lo que veo y digo,
entre lo que digo y callo,
entre lo que callo y sueño,
entre lo que sueño y olvido,
la poesía.
                    Se desliza
entre el sí y el no:
                                        dice
lo que callo,
                    calla
lo que digo,
                    sueña
lo que olvido.
                    No es un decir:
es un hacer.
                    Es un hacer
que es un decir.
                    La poesía
se dice y se oye:
                    es real.
Y apenas digo
                    es real,
se disipa.
                    ¿Así es más real?

BETWEEN WHAT I SEE AND WHAT I SAY . . .

for Roman Jakobson

1

Between what I see and what I say,
between what I say and what I keep silent,
between what I keep silent and what I dream,
between what I dream and what I forget:
poetry.
        It slips
between yes and no,
                        says
what I keep silent,
                        keeps silent
what I say,
            dreams
what I forget.
            It is not speech:
it is an act.
            It is an act
of speech.
            Poetry
speaks and listens:
                    it is real.
And as soon as I say
                it is real,
it vanishes.
            Is it then more real?

2

Idea palpable,
                    palabra
impalpable:
                    la poesía
va y viene
                    entre lo que es
y lo que no es.
                    Teje reflejos
y los desteje.
                    La poesía
siembra ojos en la pagina,
siembra palabras en los ojos.
Los ojos hablan,
                    las palabras miran,
las miradas piensan.
                    Oír
los pensamientos,
                    ver
lo que decimos,
                    tocar
el cuerpo de la idea.
                    Los ojos se cierran,
las palabras se abren.

2

Tangible idea,
            intangible
word:
        poetry
comes and goes
                between what is
and what is not.
                    It weaves
and unweaves reflections.
                            Poetry
scatters eyes on a page,
scatters words on our eyes.
Eyes speak,
            words look,
looks think.
                To hear
thoughts,
            see
what we say,
            touch
the body of an idea.
                    Eyes close,
the words open.

THE LABYRINTH OF SOLITUDE

Octavio Paz left Mexico City for the United States in 1943. In a later interview with the Mexican writer Enrico Mario Santí, the poet explained why he had felt that he needed to leave his home country at that time: "I was suffocating in Mexico. I needed to leave. I think that's why it was good to break away with my past and to go first to the United States and then to Europe. What ended? Well, my years of initiation. What began? An attempt to explore modern poetry, a reconciliation."

Paz felt inspired and refreshed during his stay in the United States, and he later looked back on this time as some of the best years of his life. In *El laberinto de la soledad*, Paz wrote of his feelings as a Mexican living in California: "When I arrived in the United States I lived for a while in Los Angeles, a city inhabited by over a million persons of Mexican origin. At first sight, the visitor is surprised not only by the purity of the sky and the ugliness of the dispersed buildings, but also by the city's vaguely Mexican atmosphere, which cannot be captured in s words or concepts. This Mexicanism—delight in decorations, carelessness and pomp, negligence, passion and

Paz in 1945, during his stay in New York City. At first, Paz struggled to make a living in New York, but he was able to read and write a great deal and to make contact with American writers and artists; he remembered the visit as among the best experiences of his life.

reserve—floats in the air. I say 'Floats' because it never mixes or unites with the other world, the North American world based on precision and efficiency."

At the University of California at Berkeley, Paz delved into the works of such modern American poets as Ezra Pound, William Carlos Williams, and Marianne Moore. But after a year of study, he found himself in need of a job. Leaving California when his year-long fellowship came to an end, he decided to try his luck in New York City.

Having gone through most of his money, Paz looked for any employment that he could find in New York. After unsuccesfully trying to join the Merchant Marine as a seaman, he found work as a translator, dubbing American films into Spanish. He continued to read and write poetry, and in the spring of 1945, he was invited to teach at Middlebury Col-

Paz visited the eminent poet Robert Frost in Vermont in 1945. Though Frost was nearly 40 years older than Paz, the two men found that they shared many opinions about poetry and life.

New York's bustling Fifth Avenue as it looked during the time of Paz's visit. Although he harshly criticized the United States for its economic and political domination of Mexico, Paz admired the vitality of North American society and formed close friendships with American artists.

lege in Vermont. During his stay at Middlebury, Paz visited the renowned New England poet Robert Frost, who was living in a cabin nearby.

Frost, then past 70, made a powerful impression on Paz, who later recalled, "With his white shirt open ... with his philosopher's head and his farmer's hands, he looked like an ancient sage, the kind who prefers to observe the world from his retreat." Though this withdrawal was a far cry from Paz's own energetic wanderings, the two men found themselves deeply in agreement about the nature of the poet's calling. As Frost expressed it: "In each line, in each phrase the possibility of failure is concealed.... That's how life is: at every moment we can lose it.... Each instant is a choice."

After joining the Mexican diplomatic corps, Paz spent five years in Paris, where he met all the leaders of French culture. Novelist Albert Camus (right) was one of the thinkers Paz admired most.

Not long after his visit to Frost, Paz was contacted by Columbia University. The Mexican poet José Juan Tablada had died that summer, and the university provided Paz with a grant to write a study of Tablada, who at the time was not very popular in Mexican literary circles. When Paz's study was published, it not only helped to establish Tablada's importance in Mexico but also created a new interest for Paz that was to last throughout his life: he began to share Tablada's fascination with Asian cultures.

Later in 1945, Paz met with an old friend of his father's, Francisco Castillo Nájera. Castillo suggested that since Paz enjoyed traveling so much, he should consider joining the Mexican diplomatic corps. Paz accepted Nájera's offer of help, and within the year, the young poet was off to Paris to begin his diplomatic career.

For the next five years, Paz lived and worked in Paris. The French city was abuzz with intellectual activity, and Paz eagerly devoured the works of the controversial thinkers living in Paris at the time. Among the most renowned were the philosopher and dramatist Jean-Paul Sartre, the novelist Albert Camus,

The French poet and artist André Breton was the leader of the surrealist movement when Paz lived in Paris during the late 1940s. Paz wrote that he found in surrealism "the idea of rebellion, the idea of love and of liberty, in relation to man."

and the surrealist poet André Breton. Although Sartre reigned over the French literary scene, Paz found himself more strongly drawn to Camus and to the surrealists. He later recalled, "When I arrived in Paris after the war, I noticed that the literary scene was dominated on one side by the Communists . . . and on the other side by Sartre and the existentialists, with one island: Camus, and another island: the surrealist group."

Paz became close friends with Breton and worked on various surrealist publications and exhibitions. In an interview with the French writer Claude Couffon, he indicated that surrealism gave him what he found lacking in communism and other political move-ments: "The influence of surrealism has had a decisive effect on me, but more as a mentality, as an attitude. . . . I have found in surrealism the idea of rebellion, the idea of love and of liberty, in relation to man."

Although Paz spent much of his time with Parisians and other Europeans, he maintained contact with Latin American writers as well. Such poets as Nicanor Parra, Enrique Gonzalo Rojas, and José Lezamo Lima were busy carving new words and ideas from the Spanish language in the 1940s. Paz saw this generation of avant-garde Latin American writers, of which he was very much a part, as bold explorers. For Paz, poetry was serious work, and the changes that these poets were rendering not only affected literature but all of humanity. In *El arco y la lira* (The Bow and the Lyre), he wrote, "Poetry is knowledge, salvation, power, abandonment. An operation capable of chang-ing the world."

Paz considered himself a laborer whose tools were words, and he claimed that he constantly read the dictionary. "I read it every day," he told Rita Gilbert. "It's my adviser, my elder brother. It's magic, a foun-tain of surprises: you look for a word and always find another. The truth about the world ought to be found in the dictionary, since its pages contain all the nouns in the world. But it's not: the dictionary presents us with a list of words, and it's for men, not only writers, to link them together so that one of those precarious associations formulates the truth about the world, a relative truth that dissolves as it is read." He especially enjoyed searching through old dictionaries where he could discover obscure connections in the web of language.

In the late 1940s, Paz began to work at a breath-taking pace on his poetry as well as on his prose. By 1950, he was ready to publish his first full-length book of prose, *El laberinto de la soledad*.

One of Paz's most widely praised books of prose, *El laberinto de la soledad* explored the myths of contemporary Mexico, as well as the poet's thoughts on the occult aspects of life, sacred apparitions, and the importance of the fiesta in Mexican life. The book contained a sharp analysis of the special relationship between the United States and Mexico in the 20th century. His distance from both cultures—Paz wrote the book while living in Paris—gave him a freedom and detachment he might not have enjoyed at home.

As a poet, Paz felt it only natural that he would have a strong interest in history. "Already at that time [when he wrote *El laberinto de la soledad*] I thought as I do now, that history is a form of knowledge set between science properly speaking and poetry. Historical knowledge is not quantitative nor can the historian discover historical laws. The historian describes things like a scientist and has visions like a poet."

In 1951, Paz released *¿Águila o sol?* (Eagle or Sun?). Using elements particular to surrealist poetry, Paz again explored his native Mexico in this collection of prose poems. But the work was also a study of language and of reality itself—concerns that appear over and over throughout his work. In "El ramo azul" (The Blue Bouquet), the poet expresses a childlike wonder as he (or a persona he embodies in the poem) steps out into the star-filled night:

> At first I couldn't see anything. I fumbled along the cobblestone street. I lit a cigarette. Suddenly the moon appeared from behind a cloud, lighting a white wall that was crumbled in places. . . . The night hummed, full of leaves and insects. Crickets bivouacked in the tall grass. I raised my head: up there the stars too had set up camp. I thought that the universe was a vast system of signs, a conversation between giant beings. My actions, the cricket's saw, the star's blink, were nothing but pauses and syllables, scattered phrases from that dialogue. What word could it be, of which I was a syllable? Who speaks the word? To whom is it spoken? I threw my cigarette down on the sidewalk. Falling, it drew a shining curve, shooting out brief sparks like a tiny comet.

In a bizarre twist, the narrator is later accosted by a thief in search of blue eyes. But the air of mystery in this youthful contemplation resounds throughout the poem.

Later in the year, Paz was named one of two Mexican delegates to the Cannes Film Festival, held each year on the French Riviera. He demonstrated his commitment to the visual arts and to his fellow artists by fighting for the showing of Luis Buñuel's film *Los olvidados* (The Forgotten Ones) at the festival. Since his teens Paz had admired the work of Buñuel, who had left his native Spain after the fall of the Republic and was living and working in Mexico. However, many influential Mexicans believed that *Los olvidados*, which depicted the brutal life of young people in the slums of Mexico City, showed their country in a negative light, and they did not want the film shown at the prestigious festival.

A scene from Luis Buñuel's classic 1951 film Los olvidados. *Many Mexicans disliked the film because of its harsh portrayal of the Mexico City slums. Paz, however, believed in Buñuel's genius and fought to have the film shown at the prestigious Cannes Film Festival.*

Paz felt it was his duty to side with the controversial filmmaker. He contacted a number of prominent French artists and asked them to attend the festival in support of Buñuel. He then wrote an essay of appreciation entitled "The Poet Buñuel"; at its conclusion, he reaffirmed the importance of all true works of art, in whatever form: "Art, when it is free, is witness, conscience. Buñuel's work proves what creative talent and artistic conscience can do when nothing but their own liberty constrains or drives them." Not having the money to print the essay, he had it mimeographed and handed it out to people at the door of the theater in Cannes when the film had its showing. *Los olvidados* did not win the coveted Grand Prize at Cannes, but to Paz's satisfaction it was widely discussed in the French press; and as Paz noted in a later essay, "With that film begins Buñuel's second and great creative period."

At the end of the year, Paz was sent by the diplomatic service to New Delhi, India. He spent four months there, deeply impressed by the spiritual sensitivity of the country. In contrast to his Catholic upbringing, which had never provided the freedom to criticize the church, the Buddhist religion seemed liberating to Paz. In *El arco y la lira*, he wrote of Siddhartha Gautama, the Indian holy man known as the Buddha: "Buddha presents himself as a critic of tradition and asks his listeners not to accept his words without first examining them. But Buddhism—at least in its original form—does not aim to explain the foundations of the world, but to offer us a means of escape."

In the middle of 1952, Paz was transferred to Japan. Japanese culture proved to be just as exciting as India's. Paz later wrote about his, or any Westerner's, first contact with Japan: "It's commonplace to say that the first impression produced by whatever contact—even the most inattentive and casual—with Japanese culture is strange. . . . Few peoples have created a style of life so unique." This quality, along with the unusual poetic forms of Japanese literature, were to inspire in Paz a lifelong interest in Japan's cultural life. While in Tokyo, Paz wrote "¿No hay salida?" (Is There No Exit?). In this poem—which shares the deceptive simplicty of many Asian verse forms—the poet seems to step outside of himself, outside of time, to view his life from a new point of view.

After Tokyo, Paz was sent to Geneva, Switzerland. He stayed there only a short while before being dispatched back to Mexico City. Although he had left

Mexico with some bitterness, he had matured both poetically and emotionally during his time away. He now felt fully prepared to face his mother country once again.

OPENING THE WAY

Octavio Paz had been away from his homeland for nine years when he returned to Mexico in 1952. Although he was received coldly by most of the writers of his generation—many of them were bitter about his stance as an outsider on political and moral issues, his refusal to adhere to any party or doctrine— Paz felt rejuvenated back in Mexico City, where he would remain for almost six years. He later said of his return: "I was reborn, and the man who came back to Mexico at the end of 1952 was a different poet, a different writer. If I had stayed in Mexico [in 1946], I probably would have drowned in journalism, bureaucracy, or alcohol."

With this feeling of rebirth, Paz eagerly began to work on many projects—including books of essays, literary conferences, and, of course, his passionate involvement with poetry. The Mexican writer Alberto Ruy Sánchez wrote that in these years "the poetic work of Paz took a course each time more innovative and experimental. His poetic adventure was opening the road even to the youngest poets who, before encountering their own voice, sometimes passed by where he passed first."

In Mexico, Paz felt closest to these open-minded young writers. He formed a close relationship with

Octavio Paz in Istanbul, Turkey, in 1962. During the 1950s and 1960s, Paz's interest in other cultures was more and more evident in his poetry.

73

the young novelist Carlos Fuentes, and together they struggled to change the artistic and literary life of Mexico. Paz also experimented in theatrical productions. With several young artists—including the writer-painter Leonora Carrington and the painter Juan Soriano—Paz founded Poesía en Voz Alta (Poetry Aloud), a theater group that was praised for its originality in drama and theatrical stagings.

Paz was also in the midst of writing a series of eight long poems, which he would publish between 1948 and 1957. Eventually these poems would be gathered together in *La estación violenta* (The Violent Season). In "El cántaro roto" (The Broken Jug), first published in 1955, he uses the image of a broken jug to represent a drought-ridden Mexican landscape. Jason Wilson has suggested that the poem can be read in an autobiographical sense. After nine years away, Paz was treated almost as a foreigner in Mexico. The desolation of the landscape is a reflection of the cultural environment that Paz encountered on his return. The people in this wasteland are now lost, without their original gods and the meanings that the earth once held for them:

> Tell me, drouth, tell me, burnt earth, earth of ground
>   bones, tell me, agonized moon:
> is there no water,
> is there only blood, only dust, only naked footsteps on
>   the thorns,
> only rags and food for insects and stupor under the
>   impious noon, that golden chief? . . .
> Where are the gods, the corn-god, the flower-god, the
>   water-god, the blood-god, the Virgin,
> have they all died, have they all departed, broken
>   waterjars at the edge of the blocked fount?

Yet Paz includes an element of hope in this long work. As opposed to some of Paz's earlier works, the poem ends not in despair but in the belief that language has the power to bring relief and joy, just as the water can cure the physical suffering of the people inhabiting the dry land and restore to them a timeless vision of the world:

> we must sing till the dream engenders in the sleeper's
> flank the red wheat-ear of resurrection,
> the womanly water, the spring at which we may drink
> and recognize ourselves and recover,
> the spring that tells us we are men, the water that
> speaks alone in the night and calls us by name,
> the spring of words that say I, you, he, we, under the
> great tree, the living statue of the rain.

Paz's anger against some of his fellow Mexican writers, whom he felt were not revolutionary enough, was expressed through his belief in surrealism. He denied that surrealism was dead, as many in Mexico contended, and he refused to abandon his vision of a new society, no matter how deaf others sometimes seemed to be to his words.

When he returned to Mexico in 1952, Paz was immediately drawn to the new generation of writers. Among them was the novelist Carlos Fuentes (right), who joined with Paz in an attempt to revitalize the artistic life of Mexico.

Paz began another poetic search while he was writing *La estación violenta*. He published *El arco y la lira*, the culmination of this pursuit, in 1956. In this work, for which Paz received the prestigious Xavier Villaurrutia Prize, he tried to address a question that had been plaguing him since adolescence: Why write poetry? In the introduction to his new book, he provided an answer: "Perhaps the only justification for writing is that it tries to answer the question we asked ourselves one day, which will not let us rest until it receives an answer. The great books—I mean: the *necessary books*—are those that can answer the questions that other men, darkly and without formulating them clearly, ask."

In *El arco y la lira*, Paz also tries to define the essential difference between poetry and other forms of communication. He asserts the importance of inspiration—the mysterious force that causes humans to write. All poets, no matter how much they may plan or scheme, must depend on inspiration and be willing to forge ahead into the unknown with no idea how a poem will turn out until it is written on the page.

To explain how inspiration works, he describes two types of poet. He begins with the poet who believes that sheer hard work is the necessity for writing a poem: "Bending over his desk, his eyes fixed in a vacant stare, the poet-who-does-not-believe-in-inspiration has just finished his first stanza in accordance with the prearranged plan. Nothing has been left to chance. Each rhyme and each image possesses the rigorous necessity of an axiom. . . . But one word is needed to complete the final hendecasyllable. The poet consults the dictionary, searching for the rebel rhyme. He does not find it. He smokes, stands up, sits down, stands up again. Nothing: emptiness, sterility. And suddenly, the rhyme appears. Not the expected one, but another—always another—that completes the stanza in an unforseen way, perhaps contrary to the original plan."

Paz then goes on to describe the other kind of poet, undoubtedly including a great deal of himself in the portrait: "Something similar happens in the opposite case. Abandoned to 'the inexhaustible flow of the murmur,' his eyes closed to the outside world, the poet writes without pause. At first, the words come too fast or too slowly, but gradually the rhythm of the hand that writes conforms to that of the thought that dictates. Now the fusion has been achieved, there is no longer any distance between thought and utterance. . . . Everything flows with felicity until the interruption comes: there is a word—or the reverse of a word: a silence—that blocks his way. The poet tries again and again to elude the obstacle, to go around it, to avoid it somehow and continue. But it is useless: every path leads back to the same stone wall. The spring has dried up. The poet rereads what he has just written and confirms, not without wonder, that this snarled text is possessed of a certain coherence. The poem has an undeniable unity of tone, rhythm and temperature. It is a whole."

In his concern with the sources of inspiration, Paz often turned to sensual, even erotic images. In *Piedra de sol* (Sunstone), for example, Paz uses the image of the feminine as the opening of poetic experience:

> your skirt of corn ripples and sings,
> your skirt of crystal, your skirt of water,
> your lips, your hair, your glances rain
> all through the night, and all day long
> you open my chest with your fingers of water

Paz saw a deficiency in the Western world—and especially in the capitalist society of the United States—because of its use of the masculine as the predominant model for society. In an interview with Rita Gilbert, Paz explained: "When North American man thinks that work, thrift, and domination are fundamentals . . . when he conceives of sport as competition and war . . . when he also sees pleasure as a form of work . . . , man is being mutilated by the masculine archetype. Western civilization should be feminized."

Despite his criticism, Paz continued to take a keen interest in North American writers and artists. During his many trips to the United States, he became close to the poet Elizabeth Bishop and the composer John Cage. One of his most memorable experiences was a visit with William Carlos Williams in 1955, at Williams's home in Rutherford, New Jersey. Williams, whose mother had been born in Puerto Rico, had translated one of Paz's poems into English, and Paz had been deeply impressed by the quality of the translation. He also loved the idea that Williams, a critically acclaimed poet, chose to live in a small town and to continue practicing medicine, his original career. "I have never met a less affected man," Paz wrote of the visit. "He was possessed by poetry, not by his role as a poet. Wit, calmness, that not taking yourself seriously which Latin American writers so lack. In each French, Italian, Spanish, and Latin American writer . . . a clergyman is concealed; among the Americans plainness, sympathy, and *democratic* humanity—in the true sense of this word—break the professional shell." Discussing the relations between Mexico and the United States, the two poets agreed that Mexicans had to bear the smothering burden of the past, while North Americans had to bear the burden of an uncertain future.

For Paz, 1955 was a pivotal year. He began to translate *Narrow Words*, a book by the Japanese haiku poet and traveler Basho Matsuo. (Haiku is a Japanese verse form in which each poem consists of exactly 17 syllables.) The success that he had with this work led to publication of his Spanish-language translations of

William Carlos Williams and the French poet Guillaume Apollinaire. Although his Mexican critics continued to attack him for his foreign-influenced surrealism, 1955 would be remembered for the publication of one of his most Mexican works, the long, circular poem *Piedra de sol* (Sunstone).

Praising this work, many literary critics compared *Piedra de sol* to *The Waste Land* by T. S. Eliot, a classic of English-language poetry. But Paz denied the comparison in an interview with Roberto González Echevarría and Emir Rodríguez Monegal: "I don't see any relation. The form is different, the vocabulary is different, the images, the rhythm, the vision of the world, everything is different. *Piedra de sol* is a linear poem that without stopping to return on itself is a

An ancient Aztec calendar stone, now in the collection of the American Museum of Natural History. In Piedra de sol *(Sunstone), one of his greatest poems, Paz followed the structure of the Aztec calendar in order to combine his personal vision with the age-old spirit of Mexico.*

circle or better yet a spiral." For Paz, the poem was a "resurrection of my experiences, my concerns, my failures, my obsessions." *Piedra de sol* would become, both for Paz and his critics, the dividing line between his early and his mature work.

Piedra de sol is composed of 584 lines of 11 syllables each. Paz, who was fascinated by numerical combinations, slightly altered the original length of the poem to equal the number of days in the Aztec calendar (known as the *piedra de sol*), which follows the cycle of the planet Venus around the sun. In this complex poem, with its many personal and historical references, Paz uses the clash of history and poetry to achieve literary revelations.

> I follow my raving, rooms, streets,
> I grope my way through corridors of time,
> I climb and descend its stairs, I touch
> its walls and do not move, I go back
> to where I began, I search for your face,
> I walk through the streets of myself
> under an ageless sun, and by my side
> you walk like a tree, you walk like a river,
> and talk to me like the course of a river,
> you grow like wheat between my hands,
> you fly like a thousand birds, and your laugh
> is like the spray of the sea, your head
> is a star between my hands, the world
> grows green again when you smile,
> eating an orange,
> the world changes
> if two, dizzy and entwined,
> fall on the grass: the sky comes down, trees
> rise, space becomes nothing but light
> and silence. . .
> . . . and we lose
> our names and float adrift in the blue
> and green, total time where nothing
> happens but its own, easy crossing . . .

The poem ends with the same words that it began with, evoking the end of one circuit of Venus about the sun and the beginning of another.

Paz and French artist Yves Bonnefoy visit the Taj Mahal, in Agra, India, during the late 1960s. When Paz was appointed Mexican ambassador to India in 1962, he became entranced by Indian culture and Hindu mythology and soon translated these influences into his poetry.

In 1958, Paz's collection *La estación violenta* was published. But it was not until 1960, with *Piedra de sol* serving as its finale, that Paz released the first poetic collection about which he truly felt proud—*Libertad bajo palabra* (Freedom on Parole). In this revision of an earlier collection, Paz gathered the strongest poems that he had written up to that point. Instead of arranging them chronologically, he organized them by theme, rhythm, and atmosphere. Many of the poems had been altered—some only slightly, others noticeably so—as Paz reworked the language, making them stronger and more resilient. And now, with his early work packed up and left neatly behind him, Paz was ready to embark on the next stage of his poetic journey.

After spending three years in France, Paz returned to India to serve as the Mexican ambassador in New Delhi in 1962. He was now 48 years old, and his poetry was being read not only in his own country but also, through translations, around the world. A new collection, *Salamandra* (Salamander), appeared in that year, comprised mostly of poems that he had written when he lived in Paris. After the appearance of this book, the International Poetry Center in Brussels, Belgium, awarded Paz its International Grand Prize for poetry. This award was the first of many he was to receive throughout his career.

During Paz's stay in India, the influence of the country on his poetry would become more and more evident. In such poems as "El día en Udaipur" (The Day in Udaipur) and "Al pintor Swaminathan" (To the Painter Swaminathan), Indian myths are referred to and explored. The leisurely pace of his work at the embassy gave Paz plenty of time to travel and write. He journeyed not only around the subcontinent of India but also to Afghanistan and Ceylon. Yet it is the Indian culture that shines through in *Ladera Este (1962–1968)* (Eastern Slope, 1962–1968), his most prominent poetry collection from the 1960s. Instead of simply dwelling on India's myths and legends, however, Paz also confronts human misery in such poems as "El Balcón" (The Balcony).

Expressions of the poet's visions—those moments of harmony and ecstasy—also appear in his work at this time. Paz was reading many books on Buddhist philosophy and religion, and these texts clearly influenced his writing. But even with all of these poetic revelations, he was still leading a solitary life. That changed for good, however, when he became attracted to a young Frenchwoman named Marie-José Tramini. Tramini was equally drawn to the distinguished poet, now in his 50th year. In 1964, Paz and Tramini married. Paz recalled that the ceremony took place "under a big tree. A very leafy *nim*. That tree was full of squirrels, and eaglets would sometimes perch

Paz described his 1964 marriage to Marie-José Tramini (shown at right, with Paz and the artist Leonora Carrington) in the following terms: "After being born, that's the most important thing that has happened to me."

on the highest branches and a lot of ravens as well."
Together the couple learned much in India, as the
poet later recalled: "In the afternoons of winter, that
garden [outside their home] would be illuminated
with a smooth light, outside of time. A light that was
impartial, reflective. I remember that I said to Marie-
José: 'It will be difficult to forget the lessons of this
garden.' Lessons of friendship, of fraternity with the
plants and animals. We are all part of the same thing."

Paz was very prolific in India, and these were some
of the happiest years of his life. He found time to read
and reread one of his favorite writers, the French poet
Stéphane Mallarmé, whose influence can be seen in
Paz's long poem *Blanco*, published in 1967.

Paz's physical distance from his country did not
prevent him from continuing his quest to open
Mexico to new cultural experiences. With three other
Mexican poets, he edited *Poesía en movimiento: México
1915–1966* (Poetry in Movement: Mexico 1915–
1966), which celebrated those poets who had broken
new ground in their country's verse. The volume
emphasized Paz's dual role in Mexican literature: in
addition to being a creator, he was also a leader to
whom younger poets turned for advice, criticism, and
encouragement. In *Poesía en movimiento*, Paz declared
his desire "to recapture those moments in which
poetry, in addition to being a frank artistic expression,
is a search, a transformation, not simply an acceptance
of tradition."

Paz's poetic collection *Discos visuales* (Visual Disks)
was released in 1968. The poems in this experimental
work, with verses based on a combination of trigrams
(a structure of three whole or broken lines), clearly
revealed the influence of the classic Chinese text *I
Ching*. His "Topoemas," first published in the *Revista
Universidad de México* (University of Mexico Review)
at the end of 1968, were even more unusual. Paz's

Paz visits with the avant-garde American composer John Cage in 1966. Always interested in experimenting with new forms and techniques, Paz wrote a number of poems during the 1960s that combined words with graphic design.

pluralism, his belief in accepting influences from cultures around the world, was especially obvious in this work, which mixed graphics and words together.

Although Paz was not the only Latin American writer to be influenced by Asian culture—Jorge Luis Borges, for example, wove ancient Chinese philosophy into a number of his poems and tales—Paz delved into Indian culture to further his lifelong goal of defining human thought and awareness. He was especially impressed by the great respect Indian culture had for silence, something he found essential for great poetry. In discussing the work of his friend the American poet Elizabeth Bishop, he praised her skill in the language of silence. "She was a master of silence, and that is very important. This communication not only of the evident things, the said things, because I think our lives are made not only of the things that are said but the things that we don't say, that we cannot say, and the job of the poet is to show it—to show the silence—and Elizabeth was a master of this difficult art."

One of the most moving events of Paz's life during the late 1960s occurred when he made a trip to London to take part in a poetry festival. Among the other poets included in the festival was Pablo Neruda. Paz and Neruda had not spoken since their dispute 20 years earlier, and Paz doubted that he would see Neruda or hear from him. However, there was a surprise in store for him, as he recalled in a later interview:

> We'd sometimes be at the same place at the same time, and I knew he would tell our mutual friends to stop seeing me because I was a "traitor." But then the Khrushchev report about the Stalinist terrors was made public and shattered his beliefs. We happened to be in London at the same poetry festival. I had just remarried, as had Pablo. I was with Marie-José, my wife, when we met Matilde Urrutia, his wife. She said, "If I'm not mistaken, you are Octavio Paz." To which I answered, "Yes, and you are Matilde." Then she said, "Do you want to see Pablo? I think he would love to see you again." We went to Pablo's room, where he was being interviewed by a journalist. As soon as the journalist left, Pablo said, "My son," and embraced me. The expression is very Chilean—"*mijito*"—and he said it with emotion. I was very moved, almost crying. . . . He sent me a book, I sent him one. And then a few years later, he died. It was sad, but it was one of the best things that has ever happened to me—the possibility to be friends again with a man I liked and admired so very much.

In 1967, Paz also published a collection of essays, *Corriente alterna* (Alternating Current). In the first section, "What Does Poetry Name?," he confronted the difficult position of being a poet in the 20th century. Although he well understood that modern poetry was often dismissed by the majority of people—even fervent readers would often avoid the complexities of contemporary verse—Paz vigorously defended the act of writing poetry: "In short, modern poetry is an attempt to do away with all conventional meanings because poetry itself becomes the ultimate meaning of life and of man; therefore, it is at once the destruction and the creation of language. . . . Those who dismiss this quest as 'utter madness' are legion. Nonetheless, for more than a century a few solitary spirits, among them the noblest and most gifted human beings who have ever trod this earth, have unhesitatingly devoted their entire lives to this absurd undertaking."

Continuing his interest in the plastic arts, Paz wrote *Marcel Duchamp o el castillo de la pureza* (Marcel Duchamp or the Castle of Purity). In exploring the work of Duchamp, the prankster of modern art, Paz revealed his own relationship with his readers: "Image that reflects the image of the one who contemplates it, we shall never be able to see it without seeing ourselves. . . . It is true that the spectator creates a work different from the one imagined by the artist, but between one work and the other, between what the artist *tried* to do and what the spectator *thinks* that he sees, there is a *reality*: the work."

Paz's happy years in India ended with the tragic student massacre in Tlatelelco on October 2, 1968. But with the resignation of his diplomatic post, Paz gained the freedom to travel and work as he wished. (A few years after he resigned, Paz was asked by Julián Ríos if he had any nostalgia for his life as an ambassador: "No, not at all. I feel a lot freer now. Leaving the embassy was a liberation. That is not to say that during the years I served with the Mexican diplomatic corps there was a contradiction between my official situation and my poetic activity. I always thought that they were two parallel, independent worlds.") In 1970, the Pazes went to England, where he held the Simón

Marcel Duchamp's controversial painting Nude Descending a Staircase. *In his 1968 book on Duchamp, Paz related the French artist's style to his own work, believing that they both created a complex relationship between the artist, the viewer, and the reader.*

Bolívar Chair of Latin American Literature at Cambridge University.

The Pazes left for Paris after the school year at Cambridge ended. He was received there with the simultaneous publication of three of his works. The literary supplement in the Parisian newspaper *Le*

Monde celebrated the poet and his work in a two-page spread entitled "Octavio Paz: The Search for Universal Truth." After Paris, the Pazes traveled to the United States, where Paz had been invited to give the prestigious Charles Eliot Norton lectures at Harvard University. Later published as *Los hijos del limo* (Children of the Mire), the lectures addressed some of Paz's most pressing themes: the contradictory interpretations of the word *modern* and the friction between the poet and society since the Romantic movement of the 19th century.

Upon finishing his year at Harvard, Paz decided to return to his country after a long absence, despite some bitter feelings that lingered there concerning his public protests over the Tlatelelco massacre. After immersing himself in so many different cultures, he found himself with a new attitude toward the political life of his own country. As he expressed it in an interview: "In the 1960s, when I returned, the important thing was to put Mexico into words. In my return of the 1970s, the fundamental thing was to reflect upon Mexico in order to change it."

RETURN

After 12 years abroad, Paz had much to reflect upon when he returned to Mexico City. Mixcoac, a small village in the days of his youth, was now a faceless suburb. It had been completely engulfed by Mexico City—now the fastest-growing metropolis in the world—within a nightmare of urban pollution and decay. In "Vuelta" (Return), Paz laments:

I am in Mixcoac . . .
I am walking back
                              back to what I left
or to what left me
                              Memory
edge of the cliff
                              balcony
over the void

                              I walk and do not move forward
I am surrounded by city . . .
Paralytic architecture
                              stranded districts
rotting municipal gardens
                              mounds of saltpeter
deserted lots
                 camps of urban nomads
ants' nests worm-farms
                              cities of the city
thoroughfares of scars
                 alleys of living flesh

Paz visits the Aztec ruins at Teotihuacán shortly after his return to Mexico in 1971. After 12 years abroad, he found the country much changed. He was appalled to find that Mixcoac, the village he had grown up in, had been swallowed up by the urban sprawl of Mexico City.

In 1970, Paz also worked on a collective poem called *Renga* with the English poet Charles Tomlinson, the French poet Jacques Roubaud, and the Italian Eduardo Sanguinetti. Written in the Japanese verse form of the title, *Renga* was an experiment in collective poetry. It was a daring experiment, for it challenged the idea poetic inspiration that required solitude and diminished the importance of the ego: the work of each poet was left unidentified.

So many years after he had first discovered surrealism in Paris, Paz was still considered to be one of the few spokesmen for the movement. Although he often distanced himself from surrealism, especially after the death of his friend André Breton in 1966, he did write a poem for the 1973 exhibition "The Art of Surrealism," installed in the Museum of Modern Art. His "Poema circulatorio" (Circulatory Poem) was painted on the walls along the spiral staircase that ascended into the exhibit. Viewers were welcomed to the paintings and sculptures by Paz's words.

One of Paz's most praised works from this period was *El mono gramático* (The Monkey Grammarian), published in 1974. This work of prose poetry, which was written for the most part in 1970 while the poet was at Cambridge University, represents Paz's farewell to India. In *El mono gramático*, the poet combines myths with his personal memories of a journey that he took with his wife to the ruins of Galta, located on the outskirts of the city of Jaipur. The monkey of the title refers to the Monkey King, Hanuman, a powerful figure in Hindu mythology who was capable of magical feats and was also the author of a grammar.

El mono gramático is one of Paz's most unusual and fascinating books. In addition to recording Paz's impressions of Galta with his insights into the Hindu myths, the book contains philosophical reflections on the nature of language and the meaning of reality

Octavio and Marie-José Paz visit with the Russian emigré poet Joseph Brodsky in 1974. Always a champion of artistic freedom, Paz warmly supported poets such as Brodsky, who were forced to leave their native countries in order to write as they wished.

itself. The final effect is to give the reader the sense of observing Indian culture from within and without at the same time.

Although he would continue to travel through the years that followed, Paz was now firmly based in Mexico City. And even though the experience of feeling "at one with the world" that he had enjoyed in India continued to influence his work, it was to Mexico and his own past that he would turn for one of his greatest poems.

Pasado en claro (A Draft of Shadows), a long poem begun in Mexico and concluded in Cambridge, Massachusetts, marked a turning point in Paz's poetry. Although this work was in some ways an extension of his earlier long poems (*Piedra de sol* and *Blanco*), in *Pasado en claro* Paz delves into his childhood and early years as a poet, revealing his youthful aspirations and influences. In a discussion with the Mexican writer Alberto Ruy Sánchez, the poet discussed not only the mood of the work but also the very nature of his poetic calling. "Time, while still elapsing, seems to

Paz's friendship with the American poet Elizabeth Bishop had begun during his first visit to New York in the 1940s. In later years, Paz praised Bishop for having mastered the "language of silence" that he had come to appreciate during his residence in India.

have stopped. It is the window that each man has overlooking eternity. One experience that the mystics have expressed very well. But it isn't necessary to be a saint or a mystic to have this experience. I believe that all men, all children, and sometimes lovers, all of us when we sit watching the twilight, or looking at a painting, or looking at a tree, or looking at nothing, simply looking at a wall, we experience those moments in which time annuls itself, dissolves: the great moments of man that is his way out. It is what I call our small ration of eternity. . . . If people had read more poetry in the 20th century perhaps they would have acceded to these moments more easily. Not because poetry creates them, but because poetry reveals them, expresses them. *Pasado en claro* is a nocturne, certainly, but at its very center the tree of midday suddenly sprouts."

In that discussion, Paz revealed his idea of the poet's role. Then, in *El signo y el garabato* (The Sign and the Scrawl), he spoke of the critic's mission: "Criticism is not part of a tradition, nor does it follow one, although that would be ideal. Criticism serves as a guide. And the best criticism is even something less: an invitation to experience the only act that truly counts: to see." In his critical essays, Paz tried to make the reader see the beauty in the works of his favorite poets and painters. Indeed, he had stated that in regard to art, "the critic is a poet who translates lines and colors into words." Since the 1950s, he had tried to illuminate for his fellow Mexicans the excellence of modern artists from their own country and from abroad.

In addition to seven books of essays, Paz released five books of poetry during the 1970s. He also published a long study on the work and life of his friend Villaurrutia, an anthology of the work of the 19th-century writer and social reformer Charles Fourier,

An 18th-century portrait of Sor Juana Inés de la Cruz (1651–95), one of the great poets in the Spanish language. In his book on Sor Juana, Paz marveled at her ability to express her genius in an age when society and culture were completely dominated by men.

his Eliot Norton lectures, and a collection of his poetry translated into six languages. *El ogro filantrópico* (The Philanthropic Ogre), published in 1979, included analyses of Mexico that continued the work he had begun in *El laberinto de la soledad*. He was also the director of the literary journal *Plural* until he and most of the staff resigned in 1976 following a conflict with the authorities. Paz, not one to keep silent for long, soon founded *Vuelta* (Return), one of the most respected cultural journals of Latin America. Both of the new journals were often in the midst of heated cultural and political debates in Mexico, as Paz continued to challenge accepted modes of thinking and governing.

After giving courses and lectures at Harvard and Mexico's National College on the 17th-century poet Sor Juana Inés de la Cruz, Paz worked intermittently on a biography of Sor Juana for the next seven years. In 1982, he published *Sor Juana Inés de la Cruz o las trampas de la fe* (Sor Juana, or The Traps of Faith). Over the course of 500 pages, Paz delved not only into the work and poetry of this exceptional woman, who had written in a time when men monopolized literature and the other arts; he also explored the art, architecture, and daily life of 17th-century Mexico City. More than the sum of its research, the book is a work of literary criticism and an engaging study of the cloisters and courts of colonial Mexico.

After so many years of hard work, Paz was now poised to reap the benefits, both literary and personal, of his lifelong dedication.

THE FIRST POET OF SPANISH AMERICA

In 1984, friends and writers from around the world gathered in Mexico City to celebrate Paz's 70th birthday. If any of them expected Paz to slow down, they were very much mistaken. His advancing age had no effect on his interest in travel or the pace of his work. During the 1980s, Paz gave lectures and readings throughout the world, including trips to the United States, India, and South America. Although he continued to publish numerous essays, it was not until 1987 that Paz released *Árbol adentro* (The Tree Within), his first collection of new poetry to appear in 11 years.

By now, much of the isolation and bitterness that Paz had sometimes felt both intellectually and emotionally from his fellow writers had dissipated. His good friend Carlos Fuentes praised Paz, calling him the first poet of Spanish America: "Child of Mexico, brother of Latin America, stepson of Spain, adopted son of France, England, and Italy, familiar guest in Japan and India, open to all the contacts of civilization, he belongs to that small group of figures (Spaniards such as Cernuda, Buñuel, Goytisolo) that assures us that the ghettos of the Spanish culture are not eternal."

Octavio Paz in the early 1980s. As he neared the age of 70, he continued his prolific output of poetry and essays. As he did so, he gained honors and awards both at home and abroad.

99

Indeed, universalism has always been strong in Paz. Perhaps it was this faith in internationalism that caused him to be showered with so many awards around the world from the late 1970s on into the 1990s. Among them were prestigious Jerusalem Prize, which he received in 1977 in Israel; the Ollin Yollitzli Prize in Mexico in 1980; an honorary doctorate from Harvard, also in 1980; the coveted Cervantes Prize in Madrid in 1981; and the Alexis de Tocqueville Prize in France in 1989. In the ceremonies accompanying the awards, Paz's dedication to literary and democratic processes were acclaimed throughout the world.

Despite all of these prizes, however, Paz was never one to be fooled by literary fame. He well understood that the modern poet is essentially an outsider. Indeed, Paz has claimed that the the dissidents—those who speak out against power and corruption—are the nobility of the 20th century. Writing about the small following of readers attained by his old friend Villaur-rutia, Paz stated: "The glory of Villaurrutia is secret, like his poetry. I don't lament over that and neither would he. He did not ask for more than the fervor of a few while he was alive. In the modern age, poetry is not, nor can it be, anything other than an under-ground cult."

In 1990, Paz finished work on a book of essays, *La otra voz: Poesía y fin de siglo* (The Other Voice: Poetry and the End of the Century). For Paz, this work, like his earlier *Los hijos del lomo* and so many other works in the preceding two decades, was a defense of poetry. He also wrote new essays exploring the relationship between poetry, history, and nature.

As *La otra voz* was appearing in the the bookstores, Paz received a major affirmation—some would say the ultimate affirmation—of his stature as a writer. The Swedish Academy selected him as the recipient of the 1990 Nobel Prize for literature. In his acceptance lecture, "In Search of the Present," delivered in Stockholm, Sweden, Paz discussed the meaning of being Latin American: "My classics are those of my language, and I consider myself a descendant of Lope de Vega and Quevedo, as any Spanish writer would. Yet I am not a Spaniard. I think that most writers of Spanish America, as well as those from the United States, Brazil, and Canada, would say the same about the English, Portuguese, and French traditions. To understand more clearly the special position of writers in the Americas, we might recall the dialogue that has been conducted by Japanese, Chinese, or Arabic writers with the different literatures of Europe. It is a dialogue that cuts across multiple languages and civilizations. Our dialogue, on the other hand, takes place within the same language. We are Europeans, yet we are not Europeans. What are we then?"

In his lecture, Paz also addressed the fading belief in progress, or in his words, "the twilight of the future." For past generations, he said, wars and tyrannies "were the price to be paid for progress." But now, history seems to have lost its reason, and people have begun to realize that, despite the benefits of technology, "it is impossible to close our eyes to slaughter, torture, humiliation, degradation, and all the other wrongs inflicted on millions of innocent people in our century." Paz had professed throughout much of his life that personal experience, not history, defined human nature. With the poetic experience as a foundation, he concluded, perhaps we could learn to live and think in the present.

In the spring of 1991, Paz—along with other Latin American writers—presented a document to the 23 heads of state gathered at the Ibero-American Summit in Guadalajara, Mexico. With ecological problems virtually out of control in Latin America— urban populations were booming, air pollution formed a permanent blanket over many Latin American cities, and deforestation was ravaging previously unspoiled areas from Mexico to Brazil at a frightening rate—30 writers joined together to sign a petition read by the Nobel Prize–winning Colombian novelist Gabriel García Márquez. The petition proposed a Latin American Ecological Alliance to confront the most urgent of the region's problems, including the protection of migratory birds and the safeguarding of human rights for native peoples. Specific to Mexico and its neighbor Guatemala was the call for the creation of a large eco-archaeological park along the border of the two countries to protect the Lacondon jungle, ravished by timber interests, cattle farming, and oil drilling.

Through the early 1990s, Paz continued as the director of Mexico's *Vuelta* magazine. In the tradition of earlier publications that he had founded or directed—such as *Taller*, *El Hijo Pródigo*, and *Plural*—*Vuelta* firmly supports freedom of thought and is dedicated to the liberty of the imagination.

Always engaged with the visual arts, Paz wrote the introduction to *Mexico: Splendors of Thirty Centuries*, the catalog for a major exhibition of Mexican art at the Metropolitan Museum in New York. He also continued his political criticism. In a 1991 article published in the *New York Times Book Review* he wrote of his vision for the future as the old Communist dictatorships crumbled throughout the world: "This is my ardent hope. Now that the cruel utopias that bloodied our century have vanished, the time has come at last to begin a radical, more human reform of liberal capitalist society. And a reform, too, of the peoples on the periphery, grouped together under the dubious title of the third world. Perhaps these impoverished nations—victims of a succession of archaic tyrannies and astute demagogues, of rapacious oligar-

Paz speaks to reporters in New York after winning the 1990 Nobel Prize for literature. Firmly committed to living in Mexico City, Paz continued to champion artistic and political freedom for all peoples

chies and delirious intellectuals enamored of violence—severely chastised as they have been by the disasters of recent decades, will find their political salvation and, with it, a modicum of well being."

As for the poet himself, he continued to live in the heart of Mexico City with his wife and to carry on the struggle for sweeping reforms within his own nation. "It's a challenge," he said of living in Mexico City, "and the only way to deal with challenges is to face up to them."

As to where Paz would go next, he answered the question in an interview with Alfred MacAdam at the 92nd Street Y's Poetry Center in New York City:

> Where? I asked myself that question when I was twenty, again when I was thirty, again when I was forty, fifty. . . I could never answer it. Now I know something: I have to persist. That means live, write and face, like everyone else, the other side of every life—the unknown.

CHRONOLOGY

1914 Octavio Paz Lozano born in Mexico City on March 31; parents raise him in his grandfather's house in Mixcoac

1930–32 Attends National Preparatory School; founds *Barandal*, a student literary review

1933 *Luna silvestre*, his first book of poetry, is published

1937 *Raíz del hombre* is published; Paz marries Elena Garro; travels to Spain during that country's civil war

1938 Visits Paris

1938–43 Returns to Mexico; founds the reviews *Taller* and *El Hijo Pródigo* with other writers

1943–45 Receives Guggenheim Fellowship; studies and works in the United States

1945 Begins diplomatic service in Paris

1949 *Libertad bajo palabra* is published

1952 Paz returns to Mexico; begins a period of prolific writing

1956 *El arco y la lira* is published

1957	Paz writes *Piedra de sol*
1959–62	Returns to Paris, where he continues diplomatic service
1962	Appointed Mexican ambassador to India; lives in New Delhi for the following six years
1964	Marries Marie-José Tramini
1968	Resigns from diplomatic service after the student massacre in Mexico City
1977	Receives Jerusalem Prize in Israel
1979	*Poemas (1935–1975)*, Paz's complete poems up to that point, is published; Paz receives Golden Eagle Prize in Nice, France
1981	Awarded Cervantes Prize in Madrid
1982	*Sor Juana Inés de la Cruz o las trampas de la fe* is published
1984	Paz receives Peace Prize in Frankfurt, Germany
1990	Receives Nobel Prize for literature in Stockholm, Sweden

FURTHER READING

Chantikian, Kosrof, ed. *Octavio Paz: Homage to the Poet*. San Francisco: Kosmos, 1980.

Fein, John M. *Toward Octavio Paz*. Lexington: University Press of Kentucky, 1986.

Gilbert, Rita. *Seven Voices*. New York: Knopf, 1972.

Hart, John Mason. *Revolutionary Mexico: The Coming and Process of the Revolution*. Berkeley: University of California Press, 1987.

Paz, Octavio. *Alternating Current*. Translated by Helen R. Lane. New York: Viking, 1973.

————. *The Bow and the Lyre*. Translated by Ruth L. C. Simms. Austin: University of Texas Press, 1973.

————. *The Children of the Mire*. Translated by Rachel Phillips. Cambridge: Harvard University Press, 1974.

————. *The Collected Poems of Octavio Paz, 1957–1987*. Edited by Eliot Weinberger. New York: New Directions, 1987.

————. *Eagle or Sun?* Translated by Eliot Weinberger. New York: New Directions, 1976.

————. *Early Poems, 1935–1955.* Translated by Muriel Rukeyser, et al. New Directions, 1973.

————. *The Labyrinth of Solitude, The Other Mexico, Return to the Labyrinth of Solitude, Mexico and the United States, The Philanthropic Ogre.* Translated by Lysander Kemp, Yara Milos, and Rachel Phillips Belash. New York: Grove Weidenfeld, 1985.

————. *The Monkey Grammarian.* Translated by Helen R. Lane. New York: Seaver Books, 1981.

————. *On Poets and Others.* Translated by Michael Schmidt. New York: Seaver Books, 1986.

————. *Renga: A Chain of Poems.* Translated by Charles Tomlinson. New York: Braziler, 1972.

————. *Selected Poems.* Edited by Eliot Weinberger. New York: New Directions, 1984.

————. *Sor Juana, or The Traps of Faith.* Translated by Maragret Sayers Peden. Cambridge: Belknap Press, 1988.

Wilson, Jason. *Octavio Paz.* Boston: Twayne Publishers, 1986.

INDEX

JOSEPH ROMAN is a freelance writer currently residing in New York. The recipient of a George Peabody Gardner Traveling Fellowship, he has studied and traveled extensively in Latin America. Mr. Roman is also the author of *Pablo Neruda* in the Chelsea House HISPANICS OF ACHIEVEMENT series.

RODOLFO CARDONA is professor of Spanish and comparative literature at Boston University. A renowned scholar, he has written many works of criticism, including *Ramón, a Study of Gómez de la Serna and His Works* and *Visión del esperpento: Teoría y práctica del esperpento en Valle-Inclán.* Born in San José, Costa Rica, he earned his B.A. and M.A. from Louisiana State University and received a Ph.D. from the University of Washington. He has taught at Case Western Reserve University, the University of Pittsburgh, the University of Texas at Austin, the University of New Mexico, and Harvard University.

JAMES COCKCROFT is currently a visiting professor of Latin American and Caribbean studies at the State University of New York at Albany. A three-time Fulbright scholar, he earned a Ph.D. from Stanford University and has taught at the University of Massachusetts, the University of Vermont, and the University of Connecticut. He is the author or coauthor of numerous books on Latin American subjects, including *Neighbors in Turmoil: Latin America, The Hispanic Experience in the United States: Contemporary Issues and Perspectives,* and *Outlaws in the Promised Land: Mexican Immigrant Workers and America's Future.*

PICTURE CREDITS

DATE DUE